MACMILLAN EXAMS

Ready for
FCE
workbook

Roy Norris

Updated for the revised FCE exam

Macmillan Education
Between Towns Road, Oxford OX4 3PP
A division of Macmillan Publishers Limited
Companies and representatives throughout the world

ISBN 978-0-230-02762-6 (+key)
ISBN 978-0-230-02763-3 (-key)

Text © Roy Norris 2008
Design and illustration © Macmillan Publishers Limited 2008

First published 2008

Designed by eMC Design; www.emcdesign.org.uk
Illustrated by Richard Duszczak, Stephen Elford, Robin Lawrie
Cover design by Barbara Mercer
Cover photograph by Getty Images / Riser / David Epperson

Author's acknowledgements
I would like to thank Amanda Anderson for her hard work and dedication, and my wife, Azucena, for her support. Many thanks too, to Frank Hodgkins, Jamie Caswell, Joe Fisher and their students for their invaluable help with piloting.

The publishers would like to thank Louise Tester.

The authors and publishers would like to thank the following for permission to reproduce their images:

Alamy pp7, 58, 66/ 67;
Art Directors and Trip p75;
Bananastock p87;
BBC Research Central (Photo Library) p82;
Brand X p73
Camera Press p110;
Corbis p35, Corbis / Bettmann pp3, 23(t), **Corbis** / Mitchell Gerber pp2, 31;
DK Images p107 (all);
Fazioli Pianoforti srl p10;
Getty pp102, 114;
Image Bank p121;
Macmillan Publishers Ltd / Haddon Davies p23 (b);
Newsquest Oxfordshire (with kind permission of the Water's family) p42;
PA Photos p95;
Stone pp90, 101;
G.P Taylor p26.

The author(s) and publishers are grateful for permission to reprint the following copyright material: Extract from 'The World's Largest Shoe Tree' copyright © Dennis Publishing January 2000, reprinted by permission of the publisher.
Extract from 'I Want Your Job: Air Traffic Controller' by Alex McRae copyright © The Independent/Alex McRae 2006, first published in The Independent 12.10.06, reprinted by permission of the publisher.
Extract from 'The Truth Behind Body Language' by Karen Hainsworth copyright © The Independent/Karen Hainsworth 2005, first published in The Independent 27.10.05, reprinted by permission of the publisher.
Extract from 'The Worst Ways to lose your wad' by Simon Calder copyright© The Independent/Simon Calder 1999, first published in The Independent 03.07.99, reprinted by permission of the publisher.
Extract from 'Where did you get that dress?' by Sally Brockway, first published in Woman's Realm 26.10.99, copyright © IPC, reprinted by permission of the publisher.
Extract from 'Keeping it in the family', first published in Woman's Realm 07.12.99 copyright © IPC, reprinted by permission of the publisher.
Extract from 'Even if I was down on m knees I could'nt give up on my animals' by Ktima Heathcote, first printed in Woman's Weekly 24.08.99 copyright © IPC, reprinted by permission of the publisher.
Extract from 'A Life in the Day: Paolo Fazioli' by Norman Beedie copyright © N.I.Syndication 2002, first published in The Sunday Times Magazine 17.11.02, reprinted by permission of the publisher.
Extract from 'The car they will deliver by fax' by Jerome Burne copyright © N.I.Syndication 2000, first published in The Sunday Times 12.03.00, reprinted by permission of the publisher.
Extract from 'Meals on Wheels' by Sheila Keating copyright © N.I.Syndication 1998, fir st published in The Times Magazine 12.09.98, reprinted by permission of the publisher.
Extract from 'Just a Load of Hot Air!' by Tom Kelly copyright © Solo Syndication/Tom Kelly 2006, first published in The Daily Mail 08.05.06., reprinted by permission of the publisher.
Extract from 'A Writer's Life': G P Taylor copyright © Telegraph Group Limited 2006, first published in The Daily Telegraph 08.05.06, reprinted by permission of the publisher.
Extract from 'Wizard Way to Oz' by Jan Etherington copyright © Telegraph Group Limited 2006, first published in The Daily Telegraph 30.08.06, reprinted by permission of the publisher.

Printed in Thailand

2014 2013 2012
12 11   10   9

Contents

1 Lifestyle

Reading

FCE Part 2 **Gapped text**

1 You are going to read a magazine article about a woman who buys clothes from famous people and then sells them in her shop. Complete the following table as you read the article.

Name of Star	Former possessions
Cher *Mel Gibson*	*shoes, jewellery, furniture, shirt*
Cher	*T shirt*
Cary Grant	*cigarette*

WHERE DID YOU GET THAT DRESS?

As a young child Marcia Tysseling would often borrow her older sister's clothes and dress up as a princess or an actress. Marcia, 38, still likes to put on other people's clothes, only now the blouses and dresses she wears used to belong to famous film stars. She also buys clothes from celebrities such as Cher in order to sell them in her second-hand clothes shop, Star Wares, in Los Angeles.

Cher tends to get rid of a lot of her things each year and we just go over with a truck and pick them up. I've met her a few times, although I've never been wearing any of her clothes at the time. I'm not sure how she'd react if she saw me in one of her old sweaters or skirts.

I love Cher's style. I have her shoes, her jewellery and even some of her furniture. They're a real bargain because I pay less for them than she did originally. **Many of my customers don't wear the clothes they buy** and just keep them as memorabilia. 1 G

I also had a denim shirt which I bought from Mel Gibson. I wore it all the time, **even when I was decorating the house.** 2 H I really liked that shirt and it was great fun telling people which famous person owned it before.

My first ever purchase was a white T-shirt of Cher's that had peace signs all over it and which I wore until it fell to pieces. But my favourite item of clothing at the moment is a black shirt of hers by Ghost. I'm a little bigger than her, so **her clothes are often quite tight on me.** 3 D It's a plain, flowing shirt that feels really nice to wear – **except when it's raining.**

4 F The shirt shrank and the sleeves, which were long, suddenly went up past my elbows. I was really upset. I had to go into the bathroom and put it under the dryer. Luckily it survived. Now I wear it just about everywhere – around the house, out shopping, at work.

Sometimes I see Cher in magazines and think, I'd like that top or dress, and a few months later it comes into the shop. If she's worn the item on a CD cover or something, I don't usually buy it because then it becomes a collector's item and **can be very expensive.** 5 A

Although my husband doesn't share my passion, he was delighted when I bought him **Cary Grant's silver cigarette case** for his 40th birthday. 6 C It's a real talking point at parties because my husband is called Michael and everybody asks: 'Why does it say Cary?' When he tells them, they're amazed.

It's wonderful to have a part of someone that you admire, that you can actually hold, look at, enjoy and wear. At the moment I've got my eye on **a very special costume from my all-time favourite TV programme.** 7 E It's not the sort of thing you can wear to the shops, but it would certainly attract attention at a fancy dress party!

2 Read the following instructions for this Part 2 Reading task.

Seven sentences have been removed from the article. Choose from the sentences **A–H** the one which fits each gap (**1–7**). There is one extra sentence which you do not need to use.

How to go about it

- Be careful with the pronouns *it* and *they* in the sentences below. In each case they refer to something different. When you make your choice, check carefully that *the whole sentence* fits in with the meaning of the text before and after the space.
- To help you do this parts of the text above are written in **bold**. Use these clues to match each sentence to the correct space.

A If it was something I really liked, though, I would buy it, no matter how much it cost.

B I got paint on it and all sorts of other stains, but it broke my heart when I finally had to throw it away.

C It's in a cloth bag and has the actor's name inscribed on the front.

D However, I like to enjoy my clothes and I always wear Cher's things until they're worn out.

E It's Dr McCoy's original tunic from the *Star Trek* series.

F I once wore it to a TV interview and got caught in a storm.

G They don't go with any of my other clothes but they still look good on me!

H This one, though, is a lot looser and fits me perfectly.

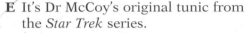

3 For each of the following definitions find a word in the text. The numbers in brackets refer to the boxed numbers in the text. The word you need is in the same paragraph.

1 famous people (eg film stars) (introduction) __celebrities__ (n)

2 collect; go and get (phrasal verb) (first paragraph) __go pick up__ (v)

3 something which is good value and cheaper than normal (1) __bargain__ (n)

4 things you collect because they are connected with a person or event (1) __memorabilia__ (n)

5 something you have bought (3) __purchase__ (n)

6 became smaller (4) __nrai__ (v)

7 extremely pleased (6) __to on etiol d__ (adj)

8 a costume you wear in order to look like a well-known person or thing (two words) (7) __to he__ (n)

4 In each of the sentences below, complete the gaps to form a phrase which has the same meaning as the words in brackets. Each of the phrases is in the text.

1 I'm going to dress __in costume__ *Batman* for Jackie's fancy dress party. (put on clothes to look like)

2 My jeans were so old they eventually fell __to pieces__ . (broke up into different parts)

3 I've got __my eye on__ a beautiful cottage that I saw for sale recently. (am interested in having)

4 It broke __my heart__ when I finally had to throw away my old jumper. (made me sad)

Vocabulary

Wordlist on page 202 of the Coursebook

A Clothes

1 Use the clues below to help you complete the grid. When you have all the answers you will find an extra item of vocabulary for number 12 down.

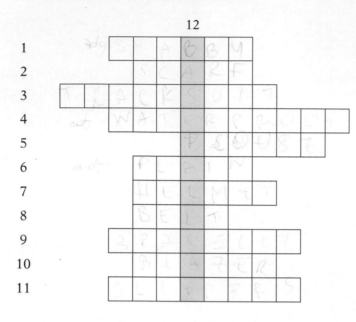

1 an adjective to describe clothes which look old and worn
2 a piece of cloth worn round the neck to keep you warm
3 loose top and trousers, worn by people during exercise or when training for sport
4 an adjective describing clothes which keep you dry
5 a shirt for girls or women
6 clothes which are simple and not colourful
7 a type of hat worn by motorcyclists and soldiers for protection
8 a narrow piece of leather or cloth worn round the waist
9 a piece of jewellery which you wear round your wrist
10 a type of jacket, often part of school uniform
11 soft shoes worn in the house

2 Use one of the adjectives from the Wordlist on page 202 of the Coursebook to describe each of the following items of clothing. The first one has been done for you **(0)**.

0 *a shabby overcoat*

1

2

3

4

5

6

7

B *Get*

Lexical phrase list on page 124 and Phrasal verb list on page 122

1 Complete each of the gaps with one of the words in the box to form a verb with *get*. The resulting verb with *get* should have the same meaning as the verb in brackets. The first one has been done for you (0).

on	off	over	away	~~to~~	out of	back	by

0 We didn't get _____ *to* _____ (arrive in) London until midnight.
1 I don't earn very much but I get _____ *by* _____ (manage to live) OK.
2 It took him a long time to get _____ *out of* _____ (recover from) the flu.
3 What time do you think you'll get _____ *back* _____ (return)?
4 He was shot while trying to get _____ *away* _____ (escape) from the police.
5 He doesn't get _____ *on* _____ (have a good relationship) with his sister.
6 You have to get _____ *off* _____ (leave) the bus at the shopping centre.
7 I can't seem to get _____ *out of* _____ (stop) the habit of biting my nails.

2 Complete each of the gaps with an appropriate word from the box.

rid	touch	ready	worse	paid	dressed	trouble	mark

1 I haven't written to Steve for ages – I really ought to get in _____ *touch* _____ with him.
2 When he was 14 he got into _____ *rid* _____ with the police.
3 I think footballers get _____ *paid* _____ far too much.
4 The car kept breaking down so we decided to get _____ *rid* _____ of it.
5 I spent the day getting _____ *ready* _____ for Christmas, buying presents and cooking.
6 What _____ *mark* _____ did you get for your writing homework?
7 My throat's getting _____ *worse* _____ . I think I ought to see a doctor.
8 Why are you still in your pyjamas. Hurry up and get _____ *dressed* _____ !

C Word combinations

1 Both the words in each of the pairs below can be used in combination with one of the words in the box. Write an appropriate noun from the box in each of the gaps. There is an example at the beginning **(0)**.

event	premiere	party	~~jacket~~	story	interview	agency	industry

0 dinner sports	_____ *jacket* _____	**4** television job	_____ *interview* _____
1 fashion film	_____ *industry* _____	**5** social sporting	_____ *event* _____
2 model news	_____ *agency* _____	**6** film world	_____ *premiere* _____
3 political birthday	_____ *party* _____	**7** news bedtime	_____ *story* _____

2 Study the word combinations in exercise 1 for one minute. Then look at the words in the box and cover the exercise. How many combinations can you remember?

Language focus

 Grammar reference on page 206 of the Coursebook

A Adverbs of frequency

For each of the following sentences decide if the position of the adverb of frequency is correct. If it is not correct, rewrite the sentence.

1 As a young child Gwen Crowley would <u>often</u> borrow her older sister's clothes. ✓

_____

2 I've met her a few times, although I <u>never</u> have been wearing any of her clothes at the time.

_____

3 Her clothes <u>often</u> are quite tight on me.

_____

4 I see <u>sometimes</u> Cher in magazines.

_____

5 If she's worn the item on a CD cover, I don't <u>usually</u> buy it. ✓

_____

B *Used to* and *would*

In the following extract from the reading text, decide whether the underlined verbs can be used with:

a both *used to* and *would*
b only *used to*
c neither *used to* nor *would*

I also **(1)** <u>had</u> a denim shirt which I **(2)** <u>bought</u> from Mel Gibson. I **(3)** <u>wore</u> it all the time, even when I was decorating. I really **(4)** <u>liked</u> that shirt and it was great fun telling people which famous actor **(5)** <u>owned</u> it before.

1 _____
2 _____
3 _____
4 _____
5 _____

Use of English

FCE Part 4

Transformations

Complete the second sentence so that it has a similar meaning to the first sentence, using the word given. **Do not change the word given.** You must use between **two** and **five** words, including the word given. There is an example at the beginning **(0)**.

0 She often went abroad on holiday before she got married.
WOULD
She _would often go_ abroad on holiday before she got married.

1 We tend not to eat much at lunchtime.
USUALLY
We _____ at lunchtime.

2 I almost always go out on Saturday night.
EVER
I _____ at home on Saturday night.

3 The stadium was always full on the day of the cup final.
USED
The stadium _____ full on the day of the cup final.

4 He phones me at work all the time, and I've told him not to.
   KEEPS
   He _keeps phone me_ at work and I've told him not to.
5 Anna rarely gets less than 70% in her English exam.
   RARE
   It _is rare that Anna_ get less than 70% in her English exam.
6 I can't wait to go on holiday.
   FORWARD
   I'm really _look forward to going_ on holiday.
7 We've been back at school for two weeks and I still find it hard to get up early.
   USED
   We've been back at school for two weeks and I'm still _not used to getting_
   _____ up early.

(**FCE Part 1**) **Multiple-choice cloze**

Read the text below and decide which answer (**A**, **B**, **C** or **D**) best fits each gap. There is an example at the beginning (**0**).

A life with birds

For nearly 17 years David Cope has worked (**0**) _as_ one of the Tower of London's Yeoman Warders, (**1**) _____ known to tourists as Beefeaters. David, 64, lives in a three-bedroomed flat right at the (**2**) _____ of the Byward Tower, one of the gatehouses. '(**3**) _____ our bedroom we have a marvellous view of Tower Bridge and the Thames.' says David.

The Tower of London is famous (**4**) _____ its ravens, the large black birds which have lived there for over three centuries. David was immediately fascinated by the birds and when he was (**5**) _____ the post of Raven Master eight years ago he had no (**6**) _____ in accepting it. 'The birds have now become my life and I'm always (**7**) _____ of the fact that I am (**8**) _____ a tradition. The legend says that if the ravens leave the Tower, England will fall to enemies, and it's my job to (**9**) _____ sure this doesn't happen!'

David (**10**) _____ about four hours a day to the care of the ravens. He has grown to love them and the (**11**) _____ that he lives right next to them is ideal. 'I can (**12**) _____ a close eye on them all the time, and not just when I'm working.'

0	**A** like	**B** as	**C** because	**D** at
1	**A** more	**B** better	**C** sooner	**D** very
2	**A** height	**B** summit	**C** peak	**D** top
3	**A** Since	**B** Out	**C** From	**D** Through
4	**A** for	**B** because	**C** of	**D** by
5	**A** award	**B** applied	**C** presented	**D** offered
6	**A** regret	**B** delay	**C** hesitation	**D** choice
7	**A** aware	**B** knowing	**C** pleased	**D** delighted
8	**A** holding	**B** maintaining	**C** surviving	**D** lasting
9	**A** take	**B** make	**C** have	**D** keep
10	**A** devotes	**B** spends	**C** passes	**D** provides
11	**A** reason	**B** chance	**C** opportunity	**D** fact
12	**A** hold	**B** have	**C** keep	**D** put

Writing

Letters and emails

In the Writing Paper of the FCE exam you will have to write a letter or an email. Some of the reasons for writing letters and emails are given in the table below.

1 Look at each of the sentences **1–10** and decide if the English used is formal or informal. Then put the number for each sentence in the correct column of the table below, next to the appropriate reason for writing. The first one has been done for you.

	Formal	Informal
Complaining	_7_	_4_
Asking for information	_1_	_10_
Giving information	_5_	_5_
Apologizing	_3_	_6_
Giving advice	_8_	_2_

1 I would also be grateful if you could <u>inform me</u> of the prices and dates of your two-week and one-month intensive courses.

2 <u>You really shouldn't</u> buy anything in the markets there – it's all poor quality stuff and far too expensive.

3 Please accept my sincere apologies for <u>the delay in responding to you</u>.

4 <u>And</u> I do think you could have phoned me to tell me you weren't coming – I wasted the whole morning waiting for you!

5 <u>With regard to</u> the number of children in our group, we <u>estimate</u> that there will be approximately 12 boys and 12 girls, <u>all aged</u> 15 and under.

6 I'm really sorry <u>it's taken me so long to get back to you</u> – I've just been so busy lately.

7 <u>Moreover</u>, when the food eventually arrived, the fish was undercooked and we had to ask one of your waiters to take it back to the kitchen.

8 Owing to the high frequency of thefts in the area, <u>we would strongly advise you not to</u> carry large amounts of cash with you.

9 I <u>reckon</u> it'll take us about two hours to get to your place, so we should see you at about 3 o'clock.

10 Can you <u>let me know</u> what time you think you'll be arriving?

2 Some of the words and expressions have been underlined in the sentences above. Match each formal word or expression with its informal equivalent and write them both in the table below. There is an example at the beginning.

Formal	Informal
1 *inform me*	10 *let me know*
8 we would strongly advise you not to	2 you really shouldn't buy
3 accept my sincere apologies for the delay in resp. you	6 I'm really sorry it's taken me so long to get back to you
7 Moreover, …	4 And, …
5 We estimate	9 I reckon

Informal letters

Informal letters: pages 10 and 11 of the Coursebook

1 Read the following instructions.

You have just received a letter from your British penfriend, accepting your invitation to come and stay with you just after Christmas. Read the extract from the letter below, and then write a reply to your friend, answering his questions and telling him what plans you have for when he comes to visit.

Thanks very much for the invitation to stay with your family for a few days after Christmas - of course I'd love to come!

I've already found out about flights, and I could arrive at 12.30 midday on the 27th December. As you know, I've never been abroad during the Christmas holidays so I have no idea what to expect. What kinds of things do you normally do then? And what's the weather like there at that time of year? Let me know if there are any special clothes I should bring with me.

2 Note that for this task you have to tell your penfriend about:

a the kinds of things you normally do at that time
b any special clothes he needs to bring
c the plans you have for when he comes to stay.

Read the model below and decide in which paragraph each of these three points is mentioned. Write each letter **a**, **b** and **c** next to the corresponding paragraph, **1**, **2** or **3**.

	Dear Roger
Beginning	Thanks a lot for your letter – we're delighted you can come and stay with us.
Paragraph 1	We normally spend the period just after Christmas relaxing at home and getting over all the celebrations. We either read or play games, and occasionally we go out for a walk in the snow.
Paragraph 2	When you're here, though, we'd like to take you to the mountains for a few days. We can go cross-country skiing during the day and in the evenings we can try out the different restaurants. The area is famous for its good food.
Paragraph 3	The temperature drops to minus 10° in December, so make sure you bring some warm clothes. A pair of walking boots would be ideal, as well as some waterproof trousers – just in case you fall over in the snow!
Ending	That's all for now, then. We'll see you the airport on the 27th. Best wishes Katrin

3 Write your own letter to a British penfriend who is coming to stay with you for the first time for **a week in August**. Include the same points, **a**, **b** and **c**, as in the letter above and follow the same paragraph plan. Write your letter in **120–180** words.

Don't forget!

Plan your letter before you write it. Use some of the informal language and linkers from page 10 of the Coursebook.

2 High energy

Reading

FCE Part 2

Gapped text

1 You are going to read an interview with Paolo Fazioli, who makes pianos. Seven sentences have been removed from the article. Choose from the sentences **A–H** the one which fits each gap (**1–7**). There is one extra sentence which you do not need to use.

A Life in the Day:
Paolo Fazioli

Paolo Fazioli makes some of the world's most sought-after pianos. His concert grands cost around £80,000. He lives close to his factory in Sacile, near Venice. By Norman Beedie

I start the day with orange juice, two kiwi fruits, vitamins, weak coffee with milk and biscuits, before driving in my green BMW 530 to the factory. Building the best piano I possibly can: that is my passion, my life's work.

I started studying piano late, but I obtained the diploma in piano from the Conservatorio di Pesaro. I had an engineering degree, too. And because my father was in the furniture and wood industry, it seemed obvious to me what my career must be. I knew there was a gap in the market, for as a pianist I had never found a piano I was happy with. [1] So I started from scratch. I rebuilt that piano 17 times before I was happy.

Now I have my own factory, I do as I please. I spend eight hours a day in the workshop, and if I see a change that needs to be made, I can make it straightaway. [2]

Each piano is born, like a human being, with its own unique character. It is the combination of good materials and good construction that gives the best results. [3] For this we use the red spruce, sometimes called 'the tree of music'. I like to choose the trees myself, in the Val de Fiemme forest. These are 150-year-old trees, descended from the ones Stradivarius used for his violins, and only one in 200 will have the natural resonance I am looking for.

[4 D] But first the wood must rest for up to a year, so that any tension in it disappears. A piano's case, too, is important. Because of the great tension created by the strings, it must be very solid, with 8 to 10 layers glued together. Then there is the iron frame – the iron and wood work against each other with a beauty that is fundamental. A piano has thousands of working parts and the strings must be able to bear 20 tonnes of tension. Then there are 88 keys to be balanced, the hammers to be 'voiced' and the strings tuned.

My 35 workers take hours over each detail, like spinning copper round steel for the strings. [5] Last year we made about 90 pianos – our best since we started in 1980, but 120 would be our maximum. Quality is my only interest.

My staff go home for lunch with their families. They are important to me. We are like a family. One boy came to us straight from jail. People questioned why I brought him in. But now he is 25 and he is getting better and better. I see him and I am happy. Sometimes, when we have made a special piano, perhaps with a beautiful inlaid case, my workers ask me if they can invite their friends in to look at it. So on Sundays the factory is open to their friends and families. Maybe 100 to 150 will come. [6]

Sadly, I don't practise so much now. [7] In the evening my colleagues and I often eat out. I like simple food: spaghetti alla carbonara, or with basil sauce. Even though I go to bed very late, I always read. I sleep well. Because, you know, when you have such an intensive day, then you sleep like a log.

A First we choose the wood for the sounding board, the heart of the piano – the flat board which lies under the strings.

B I hand them the key and leave them to it.

C I saw I must build my own, and I knew that if I built a piano that pleased me, it would sell.

D To do this they take only the finest quality wood and always under my supervision.

E It will take two years for that tree to become a piano.

F I tell myself, 'One hour a day each day,' but there is always something else to be done.

G With the big firms, to make even a small alteration can take years of discussions and meetings.

H A machine could do this in minutes, but when they do it by hand I know the result will be perfect.

2 In these two sentences from the text the word 'hand' is used both as a noun and as a verb.

*When they do it by **hand**, I know the result will be perfect.*
*I **hand** them the key and leave them to it.*

Complete each gap with a part of the body from the box. The word required in both **a** and **b** is the same.

arm	eye	face	foot	head	mouth

1 **a** He's a reasonable footballer but he can't __head__ **the ball** very well.
 b The person in charge of a school is known as the __head__ **teacher**.

2 **a** The __eye__ **of a storm** or a hurricane is the centre of it.
 b His dirty clothes and scruffy appearance caused the policewoman to __eye__ him **suspiciously**.

3 **a** They found her lying unconscious **at the** __foot__ **of the stairs on the ground floor**.
 b Taxpayers shouldn't have to __foot__ **the bill for** repairs to the palace – the royal family should pay for them.

4 **a** It's my belief that if you __arm__ **the police**, more criminals will carry guns.
 b They walked along __arm__ **in** __arm__.

5 **a** When she reads, she'll often __mouth__ **the words** without actually saying them.
 b The __mouth__ **of a river** is the place where it flows out into the sea.

6 **a** Most of the rooms in the hotel __face__ **the sea**.
 b We've only ever spoken on the phone – we've never met __face__ **to** __face__.

Vocabulary

Wordlist on page 202 of the Coursebook

A Music

Can you identify each of the following musical instruments?

1 _____
2 _____
3 _____
4 _____
5 _____
6 _____
7 _____
8 _____

B Sport

1 Write the words for the people who do each of the following sports.

Example:
surfing   *surfer*

a athletics	athlete	**e** gymnastics	
b basketball		**f** skiing	
c cycling	cyclist	**g** snowboarding	
d golf	golfer	**h** tennis	tennis player

2   Match the sports in column **A** with the places in column **B**.

A		B
1 motor-racing	*circuit*	rink
2 football		court
3 athletics		slope
4 ski		pool
5 swimming		track
6 golf		pitch
7 tennis		circuit
8 ice-skating		course

3   In questions **1–8** choose the best answer (**A**, **B**, **C** or **D**) to complete these sentences.

1 He was given a full set of golf _____ as a retirement present.
   A bats   **B** clubs   **C** sticks   **D** posts

2 Only five seconds separated the winner from the _____ in this year's London marathon.
   A opponent   **B** failure   **C** loser   **D** runner-up

3 Olympiakos _____ 0–0 with Real Madrid in the first leg of the semi-final in Athens.
   A drew   **B** equalled   **C** equalized   **D** shared

4 Second Division football _____ get paid very little in my country.
   A judges   **B** arbitrators   **C** referees   **D** umpires

5 We are expecting over 300 surfers to take _____ in this year's national surfing championship.
   A place   **B** up   **C** part   **D** competition

6 I've never really enjoyed _____ sport.
   A going in   **B** taking up   **C** practising   **D** doing

7 The home side _____ 76–75 in a thrilling game of basketball.
   A won   **B** beat   **C** scored   **D** marked

8 The players were cheered by their _____ as they came off the pitch.
   A audience   **B** supporters   **C** viewers   **D** public

Language focus

Grammar reference on page 206 of the Coursebook

A Indirect ways of asking questions

Complete these sentences by putting the words in the right order.

1 doing/have/me/been/you/telling/what/recently
   Would you mind _____ ?

2 something/can/cold/drink/where/I/to/get
   Does anybody know _____ ?

3 party/time/week/the/are/what/you/coming/to/next
   Could you tell me _____ ?

4 homework/did/the/not/me/you/to/do/why
   Could you explain _____ ?

5 interested/Friday/playing/if/in/on/are/tennis/you
   We'd like to know _____ .

6 he/living/does/a/for/what
   I wonder _____ .

B Gerunds and infinitives

Complete each of the following gaps with either the gerund or the infinitive of the word in brackets.

1 I don't mind _____ (look) after the neighbour's cat for a week, but I refuse _____ (have) it here in the house.

2 At first I was really keen on the idea of _____ (learn) _____ (speak) Swahili, but now I'm beginning _____ (think) it's a bit of a waste of time.

3 There appeared _____ (be) no one in the house. Pickering considered _____ (climb) through one of the open windows but if he did this, he risked _____ (attract) the attention of the neighbours. He decided _____ (wait) until it was dark.

4 Please stop _____ (make) so much noise. I'm trying _____ (concentrate).

5 I really don't feel like _____ (go) out tonight. I'd prefer _____ (stay) in and watch a DVD.

6 _____ (give) up chocolate is a good idea, but if you intend _____ (lose) ten kilos in three months you'll have to do a lot more than that!

7 I'm delighted _____ (hear) you're coming to the wedding. Rachel and I are certainly both looking forward to _____ (see) you again.

8 I've been meaning _____ (paint) the front door for ages, but I keep _____ (forget) _____ (buy) the paint.

9 We'd really like _____ (live) in the city centre but it's virtually impossible _____ (find) a three-bedroomed flat at a price we can afford _____ (pay).

10 I left school when I was 16 _____ (work) in my father's firm, but now I regret not _____ (go) to university.

Use of English

FCE Part 2

Open cloze: Prepositions

Complete each of the following gaps with a suitable preposition. The first one has been done for you (0).

Heavy musicians

I've never been particularly fond **(0)** _of_ heavy metal music, but my dad's a real fan. He used to go and see groups play **(1)** _____ concert all the time when he was a teenager, and when he found out that one of his favourite live bands, 'Black Purple', was going **(2)** _____ tour again, he just had to get tickets. He told me the lead vocalist was famous **(3)** _____ being a bit crazy and that he used to jump off the stage **(4)** _____ the audience. I knew they'd had a few records **(5)** _____ the charts **(6)** _____ the seventies, and the two or three tracks I'd heard **(7)** _____ the radio didn't sound too bad, so when my dad asked me to go with him I agreed.

When they came **(8)** _____ stage I began to realize I'd made a big mistake. All the members of the band were **(9)** _____ least 60 years old, they all looked really **(10)** _____ of condition and they produced some of the worst sounds I've ever heard. The guitarists were either extremely untalented or their instruments just weren't **(11)** _____ tune. The drummer looked completely uninterested **(12)** _____ everything and seemed to be playing the same beat over and over again. And as for the lead vocalist, he was quite good **(13)** _____ jumping up and down, but he certainly couldn't sing. I got fed up **(14)** _____ it all after about three songs and wanted to go home, but my dad made me stay **(15)** _____ the end.

What to expect in the exam

Prepositions are just one type of word you might have to write in the Open cloze task, which normally has 12 gaps.

FCE Part 4

Transformations

Complete the second sentence so that it has a similar meaning to the first sentence, using the word given. **Do not change the word given.** You must use between **two** and **five** words, including the word given. There is an example at the beginning (**0**).

0 Rita, could I borrow your dictionary?
MIND
Rita, *would you mind lending* _____ me your dictionary?

1 It's impossible for me not to laugh when he starts singing.
HELP
I can't _____ when he starts singing.

2 I'm going to start playing golf this year.
TAKE
I'm going _to take up golf_____ this year.

3 I don't like playing football very much.
KEEN
I _I'm not keen on_____ playing football.

4 I hate it when I'm ill.
STAND
I _can't stand it when I'm_____ ill.

5 Andrea doesn't usually arrive late.
UNUSUAL
It _is unusual for Andrea to_____ arrive late.

6 Do you know where they're going to hold the Olympic Games in 2016?
PLACE
Do you know where the Olympic Games are going _to take place_____ in 2016?

7 I can't play tennis very well.
GOOD
I _____ playing tennis.

FCE Part 3

Word formation

Use the word given in capitals at the end of some of the lines to form a word that fits in the gap **in the same line**. The word you need may be an adjective, an adverb, a noun or the past tense of a verb. All of the words require a prefix.

1 Most of what you've written in your composition has nothing
to do with the question and is therefore _____ . **RELEVANT**

2 There was some _____ about who should be team captain. **AGREE**

3 You obviously _____ when I set the homework. You've **UNDERSTAND**
done the wrong exercise.

4 He claimed he had won the lottery, though most people who
knew him suspected he had obtained the money _____ . **HONEST**

5 Derek is so _____ . You can never trust him to arrive on **RELY**
time for anything.

6 His childish and _____ behaviour often gets him into **MATURE**
trouble at school.

7 I keep telling you you're _____ ; those trousers are far **WEIGH**
too tight for you now!

8 The potatoes are _____ ; you should have boiled **COOK**
them for a bit longer.

9 The parents, who had left the two young children alone in
the house, were accused of behaving _____ . **RESPONSIBLE**

10 He always asks me what I think he should do. He seems
_____ of making his own decisions. **CAPABLE**

Writing

FCE Part 1

Letters

Read the following Writing Part 1 question and do the related tasks in **A–D** below.

You would like to go on a short skiing holiday in winter. Your friend Nick, who went skiing in Scotland last year, has sent you the following advertisement for the resort he stayed at. Read the advertisement and the notes you have made, then write a letter to Nick asking for more information.

Write your **letter** in **120–150** words in an appropriate style. Do not write any postal addresses.

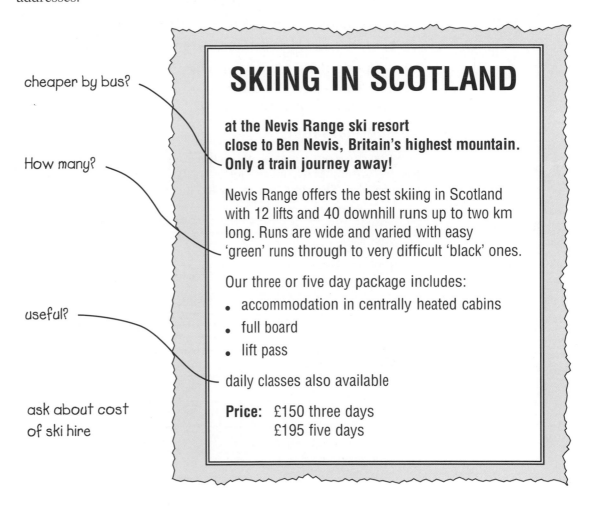

cheaper by bus?

How many?

useful?

ask about cost
of ski hire

SKIING IN SCOTLAND

**at the Nevis Range ski resort
close to Ben Nevis, Britain's highest mountain.
Only a train journey away!**

Nevis Range offers the best skiing in Scotland with 12 lifts and 40 downhill runs up to two km long. Runs are wide and varied with easy 'green' runs through to very difficult 'black' ones.

Our three or five day package includes:
- accommodation in centrally heated cabins
- full board
- lift pass

daily classes also available

Price: £150 three days
£195 five days

A Formal and informal style

In **1–9** below, decide which of the two sentences, **a** or **b**, is written in a more informal style and put a tick (✓) next to it.

1 a Firstly, as I'm not an experienced skier, I'd really like to know how many green runs there are.

 b Firstly, owing to the fact that I am not an experienced skier, I am particularly interested to know how many green runs there are.

2 a And can you remember if the skis cost a lot to hire?

 b In addition to this, could you give me some information on the cost of equipment hire?

3 a I am writing in response to the advertisement you sent me about skiing in Nevis Range.

 b Thanks for sending me the advert about skiing in Nevis Range.

4 a Finally, I only intend to spend three days skiing. I would therefore like to know whether I would benefit from having classes.

  b Finally, I'm only planning to go skiing for three days, so can you tell me if you think it's worth having classes.

5 a Thank you in anticipation for your help. I look forward to hearing from you soon.

  b Thanks for all your help. Write back soon.

6 a I wanted to ask you some questions about costs, as well.

  b In addition, I would like to have further details about costs.

7 a However, before I book, I would be grateful if you could answer some queries which I have.

  b But before I book, there are a few things I'd like to ask you.

8 a It sounds just the sort of place I'm looking for.

  b I feel it would be particularly suited to my needs.

9 a Do you think I'd save much by getting the bus from London instead of the train?

  b In your opinion, would the cost of bus travel from London be a great deal cheaper than a train journey?

B An informal letter

Now reconstruct the informal letter by putting the sentences you have ticked in a logical order. Write out the letter in the space provided. Organize the letter into logical paragraphs. The first sentence (**3b**) has been written for you.

Dear Nick

Thanks for sending me the advert about skiing in Nevis Range.

_____

_____

_____

_____

_____

_____

_____

_____

_____

_____

_____

_____

All the best

Caroline

C Building on the information given

Candidates who write good answers to Part 1 questions attempt to build on the information given by adding relevant points of their own.

Read the following three sentences and decide at which point in the letter in B above they could each go.

1 I'm a bit broke at the moment, so the holiday needs to be as cheap as possible.

2 If they're too expensive, I'll ask a friend to lend me hers.

3 I suppose it depends on the instructors – were they good?

You are asked to write between 120 and 150 words, so you would not be able to include all three of these sentences.

D Linking words and expressions

Look back at the sentences in A on pages 15 and 16 and find the formal equivalents for the following informal linking words and expressions.

Informal	Formal
as well	_in addition_
and	_____
as	_____
so	_____
but	_____

E Writing task

Answer the following Part 1 question.

You are studying English in London and you have just received a letter from your friend, Ken, who is a sailing instructor on the south coast. Read the following extract from the letter together with the notes you have made. Then write to your friend asking for more information.

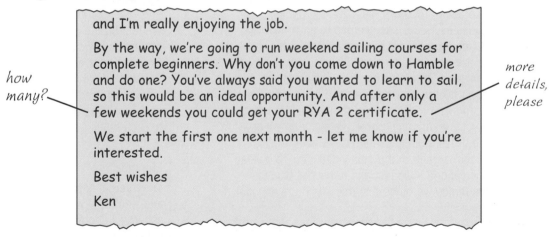

how many?

and I'm really enjoying the job.

By the way, we're going to run weekend sailing courses for complete beginners. Why don't you come down to Hamble and do one? You've always said you wanted to learn to sail, so this would be an ideal opportunity. And after only a few weekends you could get your RYA 2 certificate.

We start the first one next month - let me know if you're interested.

Best wishes

Ken

more details, please

Don't forget to ask:
- *need to be a good swimmer?*
- *accommodation - your house?*

Write your **letter** in **120–150** words in an appropriate style. Do not write any postal addresses.

Don't forget!

You're writing to a friend, so use informal language. Look again at pages 10 and 11 of the Coursebook for information about writing informal letters.

A change for the better?

Reading

Multiple matching

1   You are going to read a magazine article in which people are interviewed about technology. Read through the six texts quite quickly and decide:

  a which of the people speak positively about technology.   _____A_____
  b which of them have a more negative opinion.   _____

///////////// **Technology and you** /////////////

Like it or not, technology is a fact of life. But what do you think of it all?
June Avery asked some of our readers.

A   **Angela**

My mother bought me a microwave oven recently. I couldn't believe it – like me, she was never very keen on modern technology and there she was, buying me a microwave. I live on my own in a one-bedroomed flat and it just about fits into the corner of my tiny kitchen. I have to admit, it's extremely handy, particularly as I don't have a great deal of time to cook when I get home from work. I virtually depend on it now.

B   **Barbara**

First of all, of course, we got a PC, partly because it's so useful for work, but also, I suppose, because everyone else seemed to have one. That was fine for a couple of years, but then the kids took it over with their computer games, so we got ourselves a laptop for our own exclusive use. It doesn't take up much room, and being portable we can use it in any part of the house. After that, we just couldn't help ourselves every time a new piece of technology came out – a palm top or personal organizer, a digital video camera, a video mobile phone – we just had to have it. And the more things we buy, of course, the more we want.

C   **Carol**

Our house is full of all the latest gadgets. In the kitchen alone we've got an electric carving knife, a yoghurt maker, an automatic potato peeler, a bread-making machine and a device for taking the stones out of peaches without cutting them open. As far as I'm concerned, though, they're a waste of time. They're always going wrong and my husband keeps having to mend them. I think they're more trouble than they're worth but he seems to think we couldn't get by without them.

D   **Dorothy**

Like most people we have our fair share of appliances. I couldn't imagine living without a freezer or a washing machine; and who hasn't got a cooker or a fridge nowadays? I know people had to cope without these things 40 or 50 years ago, but the world was a different place then, wasn't it? Everything's so much faster now, and in some families men and women work just as many hours as each other away from home. We couldn't do that _and_ bring up children without the support of all these labour-saving devices.

E   **Elsie**

We're a bit too old for all this technology. A friend of ours says we should be on the Internet but I can't see why, and to be honest I'd be too scared to use it. It's all too fast for me. In the old days everything used to be so much more simple and people seemed to spend a lot more time chatting to each other.

F   **Florence**

The Internet has revolutionized people's lives, and we're no exception. We use it for everything, especially shopping. It's so much more convenient than actually going to the shops. Of course, you don't get the same personal treatment, but now that most people go to supermarkets and these large shopping centres, I really don't think you get much of that anyway nowadays. Of course, there are some things we pop out to buy such as bread or milk, but generally, once a month we make an order from the nearest hypermarket via the Internet and no more than a couple of hours later it's all packed away in the fridge or the freezer.

2 For questions **1–15**, choose from the people **(A–F)**. The people may be chosen more than once. When more than one answer is required, these may be given in any order.

Which of the people A–F

was surprised by another person's actions?	**1**
often has problems with machines?	**2**
finds it impossible to resist buying the latest technology?	**3**
is frightened of some of the new technology?	**4**
likes the speed with which things can be done?	**5** **6**
feels that technology is important in the modern-day family?	**7**
doesn't agree with someone else in the family?	**8**
has changed her way of thinking?	**9**
doesn't like the fact that people talk to each other less now?	**10**
wanted to be the same as other people?	**11**
doesn't have much room for domestic appliances?	**12**
says that the way we live has changed?	**13** **14** **15**

3 Each of the following extracts from the reading texts contains a phrasal verb. Match each verb to an equivalent word or explanation.

Barbara

1 then the kids **took** it **over** with their computer games ...
2 It doesn't **take up** much room ...
3 every time a new piece of technology **came out** ...

Carol

4 he seems to think we couldn't **get by** without them.

Dorothy

5 We couldn't do that *and* **bring up** children ...

> **a** occupy
> **b** raise; care for a child until it is an adult
> **c** be sold to the public for the first time
> **d** manage to survive or live
> **e** get control of (from somebody else)

4 Complete each of the following gaps with the correct form of one of the phrasal verbs from exercise 3.

1 We had to sell the car last year and we're finding it difficult to _____ without it.
2 A new computer magazine called *Log On* _____ last month; they gave away a free computer game with the first copy.
3 We're going to get some new speakers for this music centre; these ones _____ too much space.
4 My parents _____ me _____ to tell the truth and I'm grateful that they did.
5 When our daughter left home, my husband _____ her bedroom and converted it into an office.

Vocabulary

Wordlist on page 203 of Coursebook

Technology

Across

1 adjective meaning 'useful'; a _____ device
3 abbreviation: digital technology which is replacing video
7 a computer which is 8 down
9 having typed your document on a computer, you can save it and/or print it _____
10 you can do this in the sea and on the World Wide Web
11 preposition: _____ TV, _____ the radio, _____ the phone, _____ the Net
12 'to _____ on' to the Net means 'to gain access' to it
13 with cable and _____ TV, many more channels and programmes are available

Down

1 you need these to listen to your MP3 player
2 if you need the emergency services in Britain, the number to _____ is 999
4 an adjective to describe things such as contact lenses, cutlery and cups that you throw away after use
5 in order to change TV channels from the comfort of your sofa, you use a _____ control
6 abbreviation for 'information technology'
8 adjective to describe a device, machine etc which you can carry
10 a music _____ consists of a CD player, tape recorder, radio and sometimes a turntable

Language focus

Grammar reference on pages 207 and 208 of the Coursebook

A Articles

In the following sentences decide which gaps require an article. Write *a, an,* or *the* or leave the gap blank.

1 electric toaster was invented over _____ hundred years ago, although _____ consumers only began to show interest in it in _____ 1930s.

2 You can take _____ dogs and _____ other pets into _____ Britain but they have to have _____ passport and wear _____ microchip under their skin. _____ 'passport' is in fact _____ health certificate and _____ microchip contains _____ information such as _____ address of the pet and its telephone number.

3 When we were on _____ holiday in _____ mountains last week we saw _____ bear.

4 She works as _____ teacher in _____ school for _____ blind in Ireland. _____ school has over _____ thousand pupils.

5 Leslie: 'I'm looking forward to this concert. Have you got _____ tickets?'
Linda: 'Oh no! I've left them at _____ home. Don't worry, though. I'll get _____ taxi – I can be there and back in half _____ hour.'

B Comparisons

Complete each of the gaps in **1–10** with the correct form of one of the adjectives from the box. You may have to use the comparative or superlative form or you may not need to make any change at all.

soon	early	boring	good	careful	tired	fast	hard	quiet	hot

1 I knew the exam would be difficult, but I didn't expect it to be as ___hard___ as that.

2 Last summer was the ___hottest___ since records began, with temperatures reaching 40° in some parts of Britain.

3 There are too many mistakes in this composition. You need to be a lot _____ .

4 He was very ill last week, but I'm pleased to say he seems to be getting _____ now.

5 I look forward to hearing from you as _____ as possible.

6 That was the _____ film I've ever seen. I nearly fell asleep near the end.

7 The later you go to bed, the _____ you'll feel tomorrow.

8 We were the first guests to arrive at the party. We got there half an hour _____ than anybody else.

9 The cheetah, which can run at a speed of 110 kilometres an hour, is the _____ animal in the world.

10 Life in the countryside is so much _____ than in the city; no traffic, no crowds and no neighbours!

C Comparative expressions

Match a line of dialogue on the left with an appropriate response on the right.

1 Don't get upset. You shouldn't lose your temper with him.

2 I was in a hurry to leave and I fell over on the stairs.

3 Amazing, Andy! How did you do that?

4 Do you understand what you have to do?

5 He said he'd phone me, but he hasn't.

a More or less. 4

b That's easier said than done. 1

c He will, sooner or later. 5

d More haste less speed. 2

e More by luck than judgement. 3

D Correcting mistakes

1 Read **1–5** below and match each paragraph to one of the following inventions.

video	compass	radar	Walkman	space blanket

1 This invention <u>which</u> completely changed the lives of music-lovers around the world. At first Sony executives thought the idea of people walking round with headphones on their heads would not be a success. But however its creator, Akio Morita, always knew that the portable device, more smaller than a paperback book, would be popular.

2 This device was the most of important navigation instrument to be invented in the last millennium. Originally, sailors used the position of the Sun and the North Star to can know which way they were going, but clouds often caused them to lose their way. This invention made possible the exploration of distant lands, including America, probably the most significant of event of civilisation of the past one thousand years.

3 The first machines were built in the 1950s but for many years its cost limited its use to the television and film industry. By the early 1980s significantly very cheaper versions were introduced and have since become nearly as most common as television sets. Now viewers can watch their favourite programmes whenever they choose and as more often as they like.

4 This is made from a material called Mylar, a type of the plastic, covered with a microscopically thin film of metal. It is used to, for example, for exhausted marathon runners or for keeping mountaineers warm. The material existed in the 1950s but its production became much more sophisticated as a result of the Man's efforts to land on the Moon in the following decade.

5 The name of this invention comes from the phrase, 'radio detection and ranging' and is used for to detect the presence of objects and calculate their distance, as well as their size, shape and speed. Although originally developed as an instrument as of war, it is now used for controlling air traffic and predicting the weather. In addition to, it has important applications in astronomical research.

2 Each of the descriptions has **three words** which should not be there. Find the words and underline them. The first one has been done for you.

Use of English

FCE Part 4

Transformations

Complete the second sentence so that it has a similar meaning to the first sentence, using the word given. **Do not change the word given.** You must use between **two** and **five** words. There is an example at the beginning **(0)**.

0 My brother isn't quite as tall as me.
SLIGHTLY
My brother is _slightly shorter than_ me.

1 This exercise is much easier than the last one.
NEARLY
This exercise is _nearly easier_ as the last one.

2 There are more boys than girls in our class.
AS
There are _as few girls_ as boys in our class.

3 All the other chairs in the room are more comfortable than this one.
COMFORTABLE
This is the _most comfortable_ the room.

4 I eat more if I smoke less.
THE
The less _I smoke the more_ I eat.

5 I live nearer to the school than Costas.
FROM
Costas _is more far from_ the school than I do.

6 I did far better than Chris in the exam.
MUCH
Chris _didn't do much well_ me in the exam.

7 James earns more than me.
AS
I do _not earn as_ James does.

8 I've never known anyone as clever as Hilary.
PERSON
Hilary is _the cleverest person_ ever known.

FCE Part 2

Open cloze

1 Read the text through quickly, ignoring the gaps, and decide which sentence best summarizes the paragraph.

   a Printing on paper will soon be a thing of the past.
   b Printers of the future will use a variety of materials.
   c New printing techniques will revolutionize the car industry.

2 Now read the text again and complete each gap with one word.

Those of us who have **(0)** _____*a*_____ computer with access to the net are all **(1)** _____ to printing out information we have found there. With a single click, we can send **(2)** _____ to the printer on our desktop and obtain a perfect reproduction. **(3)** _____ next generation of home printers, however, will be printing out not just words and pictures, but 3-D objects as **(4)** _____ . If you are surfing the net and you see a picture of a doll that would **(5)** _____ perfect for a child's birthday present, click **(6)** _____ it and an exact reproduction will emerge from your domestic fabricator in a matter of minutes. Experts believe this will happen sooner rather than **(7)** _____ . They say that in just a few years **(8)** _____ now, we will be producing 3-D fax machines for less than £1,000 and they will be available in your local high-street store. **(9)** _____ machines will at first be limited to producing plastic objects, such as **(10)** _____ individualized mobile phone case. However, the ultimate goal is a 3-D fax machine **(11)** _____ can 'print' using materials such as metals or ceramics. If the technology can be made cheap, you could see a replacement part for your car emerge from the equivalent of a printer **(12)** _____ smoothly as a picture does today.

FCE Part 3

Word formation

Use the word given in capitals at the end of some of the lines to form a word that fits in the gap in the same line. There is an example at the beginning **(0)**.

The microwave oven

Perhaps the most **(0)** _____*useful*_____ and convenient of all domestic appliances	**USE**
is the microwave oven. You do not need to be a **(1)** _____	**SKILL**
cook or a **(2)** _____ genius to operate one, and you can produce	**TECHNOLOGY**
extremely **(3)** _____ meals at the touch of a button. Many of	**TASTE**
us would now feel rather **(4)** _____ and unable to cope	**HELP**
without one. The man we have to thank for this modern cooking	
miracle is **(5)** _____, Percy LeBaron Spencer, who	**INVENT**
manufactured the Radar Range oven for industrial use in 1945.	
Ten years **(6)** _____ the first domestic microwave made its	**LATE**
(7) _____ . This rather bulky contraption needed an	**APPEAR**
(8) _____ and a plumber to install it and was the same size	**ELECTRIC**
as a fridge. At over $1,000 in 1955, it was not immediately	
(9) _____ . Not until 1967, when the countertop model became	**SUCCEED**
(10) _____ available, did sales start to improve.	**WIDE**

Writing

Articles and essays

1 Read the following two Writing Part 2 questions.

1 You have been doing a class project on technology in the home. Your teacher has asked you to write an essay giving your opinions on the following statement:
Modern domestic appliances and devices do not make us happier.
Write your **essay**.

2 You see this notice in an international magazine.

Technology in the Home

Technology is everywhere today, and especially in the home. We'd like you, the readers, to write a short article telling us which **two** modern domestic appliances or devices you would find it most difficult to live without – not forgetting, of course, to say why.

The three best articles will be published in our magazine.

Write your **article**.

2 Decide which of the paragraphs below were written in answer to the article, and which form part of the essay. Rearrange each answer in the correct order and put the corresponding letters in the table. Pay close attention to the style of the language used and the linking words.

	Essay	Article
Paragraph 1	_____e_____	_____
Paragraph 2	_____	_____
Paragraph 3	_____	_____
Paragraph 4	_____	_____

a Firstly, there's the cooker, which keeps me in the kitchen for far too long. If I didn't have to cook, I could do a million and one more interesting things. But we all have to eat, and we couldn't get by on just salads and cold meat. Of course, we have a microwave, but the meals it produces just aren't as tasty as those from a conventional oven.

b On the other hand, some modern technology has made our lives less interesting than before. Food which has been taken from the freezer and heated in a microwave is not as tasty as fresh food cooked in a conventional oven. Moreover, the reason many people buy these labour-saving devices is to enable them to spend more time working, which does not necessarily make them happier.

c So it seems the things we most need are not always the things we most love.

d In conclusion, although technology has made life easier in the home, it is not necessarily the key to happiness.

e Nowadays, many people have a wide range of appliances and devices in their home, all of which are designed to make life easier. However, they also have some disadvantages.

f A love-hate relationship
Can you imagine an object in your house which you dislike having to use but which you know you couldn't do without? I can think of two, and just hearing their names mentioned makes me feel depressed.

g On the one hand, they have reduced the amount of time required to complete domestic chores. Cleaning and ironing, for example, can be done far more quickly and efficiently than fifty years ago. In addition, some inventions have meant that certain tasks no longer have to be performed. Washing up is almost extinct in households with a dishwasher, and thanks to the microwave, cooking is no more than pushing a button.

h And perhaps worse than the cooker is the iron. The same monotonous action, forwards and backwards, hour after hour, whether it's a shirt or a skirt, shorts or trousers. No one in my family likes ironing, but no one would consider wearing clothes or sleeping between sheets which have not first been ironed.

3 Look back at the answers in 2 and decide which of the features below occur in the article and which are used in the essay. Put a tick (✓) or a cross (✗) in the relevant column and give examples, if appropriate. The first one has been done for you.

	Essay	Article
Contractions	✗	✓ *couldn't, there's, didn't*
Phrasal verbs		
Formal linkers		
Informal linkers		
Direct questions		

4 You are going to write your own article in answer to question **2**. Decide which two items you want to write about and plan your article using the following advice.

Title Think of a title which will attract the reader's attention.
You might like to do this when you have finished writing your article.
Try to make it relevant to the whole article.

Paragraph 1 Introduction. Interest and involve your reader from the start. You could ask a direct question or make a surprising statement.

You could draw attention to the similarities or differences between your two items, and/or make a general statement about how important they are to you.

Paragraph 2 Talk about your first item and why you could not live without it.

Paragraph 3 Now do the same for the second item.

Paragraph 4 Conclusion. End with a short statement or a question which summarizes your feelings and/or leaves the reader something to think about.

5 Write your **article** in **120–180** words. Make sure you write in an appropriate style, using those features which you ticked for articles in exercise 3 above.

For more help with writing articles see page 200 of the Coursebook.

FCE Part 1

Multiple choice

1 You are going to read a newspaper article about a writer. For questions **1–8**, choose the answer (**A, B, C** or **D**) which you think fits best according to the article.

A writer's life: G P Taylor

J K Rowling may be responsible for the revival of fantasy fiction. But her contemporary rivals, many of whom have benefited from her success, seem reluctant to give her credit for starting a trend. Philip Pullman, for example, points out that *Northern Lights*, the first volume in his trilogy *His Dark Materials*, was published a year before Harry Potter's adventures began. So it comes as a surprise when G P Taylor concedes that he only wrote a novel because of the enormous popularity of Harry Potter.

Taylor is the Yorkshire vicar who sold his motorbike to self-publish 2,000 copies of his first novel, *Shadowmancer*, a book that was subsequently picked up by publishers Faber & Faber and got to number one in the New York Times bestseller list. His novels conjure up dark, **chilling** worlds in which the supernatural threatens to take over, yet he describes his life as a writer in flatly functional terms. For example, he is able to name the exact day that he became a novelist: March 21, 2002. 'It was one of those **seminal** moments in my life. Harry Potter was becoming very popular. And I thought, "This woman's written a book. I might write one." '

'I got a copy of Harry Potter, counted the number of words that were on the page, measured the width of the margin, counted the number of chapters in the book, how many pages were in the book and set my computer screen up so that it would have 468 words on the page. My chapters were the same length as the Harry Potter chapters; I thought, "This must be how you write a book." '

The Harry Potter formula has its faults, of course. Stephen King was once asked what he thought of Rowling's novels. Were they 'thought-provoking'?
line 35 King thought not. But did that matter, he wondered, in a 'fantasy-adventure aimed primarily at children and published in the heart of the summer vacation'? His conclusion was **unequivocal**: 'Of course not. What kids on summer vacation want – and probably deserve – is simple, uncomplicated fun.'

Shadowmancer is a simple and uncomplicated fantasy – and Taylor, who is his own most effective critic, makes few further claims for the novel. 'It's a great story, but if I'd written it now, it would be a completely different book. In many ways, it's a **clumsy** classic. There are a lot of things in there that I would get rid of. And yet, I think that's the big attraction. It's because it's an incredible adventure story, written by a non-writer, just a storyteller.'

Taylor returns to this distinction between writing and storytelling a number of times, distancing himself from grand and **lofty** ideas of the novelist's purpose. He describes himself as a 'fairly uneducated, council-house kid' who ran away to London as a teenager, 'a bit of a chancer, with ideas above his station'. He read Dickens, lots of Orwell – 'they were **trendy** books to read' – and Kerouac. But he is uncomfortable talking at any length about favourite novels or influences beyond Rowling: 'I have not read all that many books. I'm not, you know, a very **literate** person.'

Taylor was a rock-music promoter in his twenties and remains a showman, happiest in front of a crowd. He describes the talks he gives in schools and at book festivals, dressed up as a sea captain or as an 18th-century highwayman in a long black coat. 'You're using your face, you're using your body, you're acting out what you're doing.' The business of putting his thoughts in writing can be problematic in comparison. As a storyteller, in order to demonstrate shock or alarm to an audience he will 'pause between sentences and show a wide-eyed, staring face. But to describe that in English … '

This impatience with the limitations of language can be a positive asset: in *Tersias*, Taylor's new fantasy, the speed of the narrative and the scale of the events that overwhelm the characters mean there is no time line 78 for the story to get bogged down. That said, it is unusual to hear a writer speak in such a **dismissive** way of his craft. *Shadowmancer* has been taken on by Universal Pictures, and Taylor does nothing to hide the fact that he thinks 'the movie's more exciting than the book'.

1 The writer says that many fantasy fiction writers would not agree that
   A they have copied their ideas from J K Rowling.
   B J K Rowling's success has contributed to their own.
   C fantasy fiction will remain fashionable for many years.
   D J K Rowling is a writer of fantasy fiction in the true sense.

2 The writer is surprised by
   A the success of Taylor's books.
   B the short time Taylor has been a writer.
   C the number of books Taylor has published.
   D Taylor's reasons for writing his first book.

3 What aspect of the Harry Potter books does Taylor admit to imitating?
   A the writing style
   B the storylines
   C the layout
   D the cover design

4 What does 'that' refer to in line 35?
   A the Harry Potter formula
   B the novels' target audience
   C the timing of the novels' publication
   D the novels' failure to make people think

5 What does Taylor say about *Shadowmancer*?
   A He is aware of its limitations.
   B He did not write all of it himself.
   C He is going to write a revised edition.
   D It does not deserve the praise it receives.

6 What opinion does Taylor have of himself?
   A He is very proud of his achievements as a writer.
   B He thinks he is a better writer than J K Rowling.
   C He does not regard himself as a serious novelist.
   D He feels he deserves greater recognition.

7 What do we learn about the talks Taylor gives?
   A He enjoys them more than being a promoter.
   B He couldn't do them without dressing up.
   C He finds them easier than writing.
   D He likes shocking people.

8 What does the writer mean by 'there is no time for the story to get bogged down' (line 78)?
   A The story moves on too quickly.
   B The plot is never prevented from developing.
   C Emotions are not dealt with in sufficient detail.
   D The story is not always as exciting as it could be.

2 Match the words in **bold** in the text with the following meanings. Use the context to help you.

   a expressed very clearly and firmly _____
   b important and having a great influence _____
   c showing that you think something is not important _____
   d frightening _____
   e careless and unskilful _____
   f intelligent and well-educated _____
   g modern and fashionable _____
   h noble and important

Vocabulary

Wordlist on page 203 of the Coursebook

A Cinema and films

Use the clues below to help you complete the grid with words related to cinema and films. When you have all the answers you will find an extra item of vocabulary for number 11 down.

1 the people who act in a film
2 the story of a film
3 actors wear this, sometimes changing their appearance completely
4 a part of a film in which the action occurs in one place at one time, eg a love _____ , an action _____
5 a film which is intended to make you laugh
6 special _____ are unusual images or sounds created by using special techniques
7 another word for 'role'
8 a man who performs a dangerous piece of action in a film instead of the actor
9 a box _____ hit is a film which is very successful
10 a film that has a similar story and title to a film made earlier

B Expressions with *take*

Lexical phrase list on page 125 and Phrasal verb list on page 123

Complete the gaps with an appropriate word from the box. In **1–6** pay special attention to the prepostions in bold.

advice	risk	interest	notice	blame
courage	pity	care	offence	joke

1 He takes a very keen _____ **in** music and often goes to concerts.
2 Don't say anything negative about her hair; she's very sensitive and might take _____ **at** your remarks.
3 I was walking along a country road in the rain when a driver took _____ **on** me and stopped to give me a lift.
4 If a team loses, it's normally the manager who takes the _____ **for** the defeat and not the players.
5 Our neighbour has agreed to take _____ **of** the dogs while we're on holiday.
6 The doctor told her to stop smoking, but she didn't take any _____ **of** him. She still smokes 30 a day.
7 Although she really wanted to study archaeology, she took her parents' _____ and went to law school.
8 Jamie likes making fun of other people but he can't take a _____ himself. He gets so angry.
9 It took a lot of _____ to ride his motorbike again after the accident.
10 She was taking a big _____ when she changed career, but fortunately everything went well and she really likes her new job.

C Phrasal verbs with *take*

Complete each of the gaps with an appropriate particle.

1 She takes _____ her father; they're both as disorganized as each other.
2 I'd love to take _____ golf, but it's such an expensive sport.
3 We haven't really taken _____ the new boss; he's a little too formal for us.
4 Our maths teacher, Mrs Hill, is going to have a baby so Mr Bennett is taking _____ until she comes back.
5 They've taken _____ another receptionist at work; Alison couldn't manage on her own.
6 I had to stop going to yoga classes; they were taking _____ too much of my time.

Language focus

Grammar reference on pages 208 and 209 of the Coursebook

A Tenses

1 Complete each of the gaps with an appropriate past tense form of the verb in brackets. Choose from the past simple, past continuous, past perfect simple and past perfect continuous.

1 Susana _had_ ___ (live) in Germany for three months when she _started_ ___ (start) going out with Reiner. At that time he _was training_ (train) to be a teacher and she _____ (meet) him at a college disco.

2 When I _____ (hear) about the motorway accident on the radio, I immediately _____ (phone) my son to check that he _____ (get) back safely. He _____ (tell) me he _____ (take) a different route home.

3 We _____ (watch) a particularly romantic scene of a film at the cinema when my boyfriend's mobile phone _____ (go) off. He _____ (forget) to switch it off.

4 By the time we _____ (get) to the party they _____ (eat) all the food. In fact, it was so late that most of the guests _____ (already/leave) and only two or three people _____ (still/dance).

2 Complete the gaps in this story with the verbs in the box. Put the verbs in an appropriate past tense form.

go	hold	wait	tell	take	get
pass	sit	finish	drive	be	start

When I (1) _____ my dad that I (2) _____ all my exams, he (3) _____ me to our local drive-through McDonalds to celebrate. While we (4) _____ at the window for some more chips to be cooked, I (5) _____ to the toilet inside the restaurant to wash my hands. Once I (6) _____ , I rushed outside, jumped into the car and (7) _____ eating the chips that my dad (8) _was holding_ in his hand. It was then that I heard an unfamiliar, and angry-sounding cough. I turned to discover that it wasn't my dad in the driving seat but a rather red-faced man; I (9) _was_ _____ into the wrong car! My dad (10) _had_ already _____ away from the window where they serve the food and he (11) _was sitting_ in the car a short distance away, laughing at me. Needless to say, I didn't think it (12) _____ very funny!

B *So* and *such*

Complete the second sentence so that it has a similar meaning to the first sentence, using the word given. **Do not change the word given.** You must use between **two** and **five** words, including the word given.

1 We had such a lot of homework to do at the weekend!
so
We had _____ so much homework _____ to do at the weekend!

2 I thought there would be more people here.
so
I didn't think there would be _____ so few people _____ here.

3 The food was so delicious that I couldn't stop eating.
such
It was _____ such a deli. food that _____ I couldn't stop eating.

4 I enjoyed myself so much I didn't want to come home.
good
I had _____ such a very good _____ time I didn't want to come home.

5 It was such an interesting book that I stayed up all night to finish it.
so
I was _____ so _____ that I stayed up all night to finish it.

C **Linking words**

In **1–6** underline the most suitable linking word or expression.

1 Last summer we stayed in an apartment near the beach *during/for/in* three weeks.
2 *As/During/Whereas* I was walking to school this morning, I found a £1 coin.
3 I looked everywhere for my glasses. *In the end/At the end/At last* I had to buy a new pair.
4 You're here *by the time/at the end/at last*! Where have you been? We were worried.
5 *Afterwards/After/After that* she'd taken the dog for a walk, she made a cup of tea.
6 'I saw the new Matt Damon film last night.' 'What did you do *afterwards/after/at last*?'

Use of English

FCE Part 3

Word formation: Adjectives ending in *-ing* and *-ed*

Use the word given in capitals at the end of some of the lines to form a word that fits in the gap **in the same line**.

The word you require may be an adjective or an adverb. It might be positive or negative.

1 *Scream* was probably the most _____ film I've ever seen. **FRIGHT**

2 I get so _____ when my dad starts singing. **EMBARRASS**

3 As the day of the exam approached, Karen became _____ nervous. **INCREASE**

4 a I think I'll go straight to bed. It was a very _____ journey. **TIRE**
b Yes, you must be _____ . **EXHAUST**

5 I didn't really enjoy the film. The special effects were OK but the plot was rather dull and _____ . **INTEREST**

6 Johnny Depp is not one of my favourite actors but he gave a _____ good performance in *Sleepy Hollow*. **SURPRISE**

7 You look a little _____ . Don't you understand what you have to do in this exercise? **CONFUSE**

8 It was quite _____ to read so many negative reviews of the film. Critics wrote that the main characters were _____ , but personally, I was very _____ by the quality of the acting and would certainly recommend the film to other people. **ANNOY** **CONVINCE** **IMPRESS**

FCE Part 1

Multiple-choice cloze

For questions **1–12**, read the text below and decide which answer (**A**, **B**, **C** or **D**) best fits each gap. There is an example at the beginning (**0**).

A lucky break

Actor Antonio Banderas is (**0**) _____*used*_____ to breaking bones, and it always seems to happen when he's (**1**) _____ sport.

In the film *Play it to the Bone*, he (**2**) _____ the part of a middleweight boxer alongside Woody Harrelson. During the making of the film Harrelson kept complaining that the fight (**3**) _____ weren't very convincing, so one day he suggested that he and Banderas should have a fight for real. The Spanish actor wasn't (**4**) _____ on the idea at first, but he was (**5**) _____ persuaded by his co-star to put on his gloves and climb into the boxing ring. However, when he realized how seriously his (**6**) _____ was taking it all, he began to regret his decision to fight. And then in the third round, Harrelson hit Banderas (**7**) _____ hard in the face that he actually broke his nose.

He was (**8**) _____ of the time he broke his leg during a football match in his native Malaga. He had always (**9**) _____ of becoming a soccer star, of performing in front of a big crowd, but doctors told him his playing days were probably over. 'That's when I decided to take (**10**) _____ acting; I saw it as (**11**) _____ way of performing, and achieving recognition. What happened to me on that football (**12**) _____ was, you might say, my first lucky break.'

0	**A** familiar	**B** <u>used</u>	**C** normal	**D** annoyed
1	**A** showing	**B** making	**C** doing	**D** losing
2	**A** plays ✓	**B** does	**C** gives	**D** fights
3	**A** actions	**B** matches	**C** scenes	**D** stages
4	**A** interested	**B** keen	**C** enthusiastic	**D** happy
5	**A** lastly	**B** eventually	**C** at the end	**D** after
6	**A** competitor	**B** contender	**C** opponent	**D** participant
7	**A** very	**B** more	**C** such	**D** so
8	**A** remembered	**B** reminded	**C** recorded	**D** replayed
9	**A** hoped	**B** pretended	**C** dreamed	**D** looked forward
10	**A** up	**B** on	**C** to	**D** over
11	**A** further	**B** additional	**C** different	**D** another
12	**A** match	**B** pitch	**C** court	**D** course

Writing

Essays: Advantages and disadvantages

1 **a** Read the following Writing Part 2 question and then follow the instructions in **b** below.

You have recently had a class discussion comparing films and books. Now your teacher has asked you to write an essay, giving your opinion on the following statement:

It is better to read a book than see a film version of the book.

Write your **essay** in **120–180** words.

b Read one student's plan and notes below and then the essay she wrote. As you read the essay put a tick (✓) next to those points in the notes which she decided to include in her answer. One of the points has already been ticked.

Essay
Book vs Film version

Plan
Paragraph 1   Introduction
Paragraph 2   Advantages of book and disadvantages of film version
Paragraph 3   Advantages of film and disadvantages of book
Paragraph 4   Conclusion

Advantages and Disadvantages

Book	Film
Advantages of book	**Advantages of film version**
can read anywhere and at any time	visual – makes story more memorable
good for mind – you use imagination ✓	can improve a story and make it more interesting
can learn new words in your own language	special effects – all scenes in book are possible
more entertainment from a book – lasts long time	more elements in a film; music, colour, actors/actresses
can read a book many times	can see a film many times
Disadvantages of book	**Disadvantages of film**
too much effort needed	film not always good interpretation
not everyone can read	too much violence
	film cuts and changes to story

Nowadays, many people prefer going to cinema to reading the same story in a book. Both forms of entertainment have their advantages and disadvantages.

In the one hand, books help developing your imagination. You can decide what do the characters and places in the story looks like, whereas the film only gives you one interpretation, which may not be the best. Furthermore, the enjoyment from a book lasts more longer than from a film, and you can read it wherever and whenever you want. Another disadvantage of films is that they cut sometimes the most interested parts of the book, or change the story completely.

On the other hand, films are very visual, and this makes the story more memorable. Moreover, special effects are such good now that the most scenes of a book can to be shown on the screen. Besides this, some people prefer watching the film version because it takes less effort that reading.

On balance, I think always it is better to read the story first. After you can see it at the cinema if you want compare.

2 **a** Read the examiner's comments on the example essay and then follow the instructions in **b**.

> *Strong Points*
> *This is clearly a well planned answer. The ideas are grouped logically into paragraphs and a number of linking words have been used to connect the different points. The essay is written in an appropriately formal style and there is a good range of vocabulary.*
>
> *Weak Points*
> *There are a number of grammatical errors throughout the essay.*

b Read the student's essay again and correct the mistakes she has made. There are 15 mistakes altogether. Pay particular attention to the following areas of grammar:

- verb forms
- use of gerund and infinitive
- comparative forms
- position of frequency adverbs
- use of articles
- *so/such*
- adjectives ending in *-ing/-ed*
- prepositions

3 **a** Read the following Writing Part 2 question. Read the advice in **b** before you write your answer.

You have recently had a class discussion comparing DVD and the cinema. Now your teacher has asked you to write an essay, giving your opinion on the following statement:

It is better to watch a film at home on DVD than at the cinema.

Write your **essay** in **120–180** words.

b Before you write your answer make sure you plan what you are going to say first. You should:

- Write a paragraph plan giving a general idea of what you intend to include in each paragraph. Here is a possible plan:

  Paragraph 1   Introduction: general statement
  Paragraph 2   Advantages of DVD and disadvantages of cinema
  Paragraph 3   Advantages of cinema and disadvantages of DVD
  Paragraph 4   Conclusion

- Make a list of the advantages and disadvantages of watching films at home on DVD and at the cinema.

Advantages of DVD	Advantages of cinema
eg more comfortable watching a film at home	
Disadvantages of DVD	**Disadvantages of cinema**

- Decide which of these points you are going to include in your answer. Write your essay following your paragraph plan.

Don't forget!

- Connect your ideas using linking devices: page 35 in the Coursebook has a selection of these.
- Check your work for mistakes when you have written your essay: use the checklist in **2b** above.

5 Doing your duty

Reading

Multiple matching

1   You are going to read a newspaper article written by an air traffic controller about her job. For questions **1–15**, choose from the paragraphs (**A–F**). The paragraphs may be chosen more than once. When more than one answer is required, these may be given in any order.

Which paragraph mentions the following?

the need for perseverance	**1**
activity during rest periods	**2**
a common misconception	**3**
the importance of being able to work with others	**4**
the variety of possible career paths open to controllers	**5**
a source of personal satisfaction	**6** **7**
the advantage of the predictability in the working hours	**8**
the writer's previous experience in a related field	**9**
informing others of changes	**10**
the need for concentration	**11** **12**
receiving individual on-the-job guidance	**13**
variety within the same job	**14** **15**

Air Traffic Controllers

Sonia Avogadro, 31, is an area controller at the London Terminal Control Centre, West Drayton, which controls air space in South-East England.

A   My job is about giving instructions and any other relevant information to aircraft, so they can fly as quickly and safely as possible. I work on air traffic flying into Gatwick, organizing the planes into a neat sequence so they all come in one after another. I'm in constant radio contact with the pilots, keeping them up-to-date on the weather and any unusual conditions or alterations in flight plans. The main thing I need to monitor is the level or altitude I want them to fly at. A lot of people think air-traffic controllers work in a control tower, but in fact, only 20 per cent do. They're the ones who deal with take-offs and landings. Most of us work at area control centres away from the airport.

B   I work in shifts on radar for up to two hours, then I always have a half-hour break, where I'll move around and give my eyes a good rub. The breaks are for safety purposes. I suppose that working shifts might not suit everybody. Because it's a 24-hour business, there's a lot of getting up early and night shifts. We work a repetitive roster – two mornings, two afternoons, then two nights – so there are six night-shifts a month. The good thing is that the shift pattern is always the same, so at least you can plan your life around it.

C   The busier it is, the more you have to focus, but you really feel like you've achieved a lot. And it's a job that means something – you're looking after people's safety, so there's a real consequence to what you do. I really like the fact that it's always different. You might be working with completely different people, traffic and weather conditions every day. And at the end of your shift, you take your headset off and that's it. You don't have to take the job home with you.

34

D You've got to be the sort of person who can really focus on the task in hand, and process large amounts of complex data. Because very complicated air traffic situations can happen extremely quickly, you've got to be calm, stay on the ball, and react very quickly. You also need excellent spatial awareness. And a key quality in the job is the need to be a good team player, someone who can get on with a lot of different people.

E I was an air hostess for a while after university, so I've seen the other side of the business. One day I went up to the control tower for a visit, and thought the job looked fascinating. So I applied, and luckily I got a place to train. You have to spend up to 12 months at a college of air-traffic control, using super hi-tech computer simulators, so it's almost like working in a real airspace environment. Once you graduate from the college, you get posted to a unit where

you do more practical training, with the help of a mentor, for six months to two years. And when that's finished, you have to sit a final exam. I'd say that if you decide to apply, stick with it and be prepared for some very tough training. It's not a walk in the park, but it's very rewarding once you get through it.

F You get paid £10,000 while you're training at the college, and once you're fully qualified you could progress to earning up to £85,000. There are lots of different job options at the control centres – supervisors, watch managers. You could become an instructor at the college or you could just carry on working as a tower or radar controller, expanding your repertoire and working on different airspace areas.

2 Write the name of the person or machine formed from each of the verbs on the left. Use the appropriate suffix, either **-er** or **-or**, and make any other changes which are necessary. All the words appear in the text. There is an example at the beginning **(0)**.

Verb	Person or machine
0 control	_controller_
1 play	
2 compute	
3 simulate	
4 supervise	
5 manage	
6 instruct	

3 Now use the same suffixes to form the name of the person or machine from the following verbs.

Verb	Person or machine
0 read	_reader_
1 scan	
2 calculate	
3 advise	
4 invent	
5 present	
6 demonstrate	
7 compete	
8 photocopy	
9 research	
10 spectate	

Vocabulary

Wordlist on pages 203 and 204 of the Coursebook

A Jobs crossword

Across

This person ...
1 takes away people's rubbish
6 makes and sells bread and cakes
8 cuts people's hair
9 cooks in a restaurant or hotel
11 looks after the financial matters of a person or company

Down

This person ...
2 helps you to pass FCE
3 serves people with food and drink in a restaurant
4 gives advice to people about law and represents them in court
5 cuts up and sells meat
7 operates on people
10 treats sick or injured animals

B Questions and answers

1 Match a question in column **A** with an appropriate answer in column **B**.

A	B
1 Do you have a well-paid job?	**a** Yes, I have to make important decisions.
2 Is your job challenging?	**b** No, I have nothing to complain about.
3 Is it a responsible job?	**c** Yes, I have to treat everyone equally.
4 Do you have to be fair?	**d** No, I'll probably go on working.
5 Is fitness a requirement?	**e** Yes, I earn a good living.
6 Do you need artistic skills?	**f** No, physical strength isn't necessary.
7 Have you ever been on strike?	**g** Yes, it requires a great deal of hard work.
8 Will you retire when you're 65?	**h** No, it's not a particularly creative job.

2 Which of the following jobs might the person being interviewed in exercise 1 have? More than one answer may be possible.

firefighter	cook	judge	accountant	police officer
civil servant	surgeon	politician	architect	company director

C Expressions with *work*

In **1–7** below write the correct form of the verb *work* in the first gap and one of the words or expressions from the box in the second gap.

full-time	long hours	overtime	for myself
flexitime	part-time	my way up	shifts

1 I _____ ten hours _____ last week and earned £150 on top of my normal salary.

2 I've always _____ _____; I couldn't imagine not being my own boss.

3 You should be prepared _____ _____ as an accountant; eight in the morning till eight in the evening is not uncommon.

4 I'm _____ _____ at the moment; four hours instead of the normal eight. I'll probably go back to _____ _____ when John's old enough to go to school.

5 I'd quite like _____ _____; if you oversleep your boss doesn't get angry, and if you want to leave work early, you can.

6 My husband's a police officer so he _____ _____. He prefers working nights; that way he gets to see more of the kids.

7 I've succeeded in _____ _____ to the top of this company; from messenger boy to managing director in 15 years.

Language focus

Grammar reference on pages 209 and 210 of the Coursebook

Obligation, necessity and permission

1 Complete the gaps with the correct form of one of the following verbs. In some cases more than one answer may be possible.

must	have to	need to	should

1 I know it's not my business, but if you're not feeling very well, then I think you _____ take the day off work.

2 We were planning to go out tonight but I _____ finish writing this report for my boss instead.

3 If you feel you _____ look up any words in the text, use an English–English dictionary.

4 I _____ remember to get some eggs on the way home from work tonight. I want to make a cake.

5 _____ write a story about ourselves or can we write one about someone we know?

6 I'm sorry I'm a bit late – I _____ go to a meeting and it lasted longer than I expected.

7 I've told you before, you _____ hand in your homework to me on time – I don't want _____ tell you again!

8 You really _____ try and stop biting your nails. They look so ugly like that.

2 Complete the two gaps in each sentence with the following pairs of words. The first one has been done for you.

| needn't/must shouldn't/must can't/must ~~can/must~~ can/should can/can't |

1 **a:** Is it OK if I go to London with my friends at the weekend, Mum?
  b: You ___can___ go if you want to, but you ___must___ phone me when you get there.

2 **a:** Are you sure it's OK to come in here?
  b: Well, we _____ really be here, but I _____ just show you this.

3 **a:** Could I borrow an atlas?
  b: Well, you _____ certainly have a look at it here, but you _____ take it home with you, I'm afraid.

4 **a:** Do I have to write the date on this piece of work?
  b: No, you _____ write the date, but you _____ remember to put your name.

5 **a:** Could I take the dog for a walk?
  b: Yes, of course you _____ , but I think you _____ wear your boots, don't you? It's very wet outside.

6 **a:** My parents won't let me go and see that film.
  b: Well, if you _____ see it now, you _____ try and see it when you're older.

Use of English

FCE Part 4

Transformations

Complete the second sentence so that it has a similar meaning to the first sentence, using the word given. **Do not change the word given.** You must use between **two** and **five** words, including the word given. There is an example at the beginning (**0**).

0 It isn't necessary to bring your Coursebook to the class tomorrow.
  NEED
  You ___don't need to bring___ your Coursebook to the class tomorrow.

1 I'm glad smoking is prohibited on public transport.
  ALLOWED
  I'm glad you _____ on public transport.

2 What's their expected time of arrival?
  SUPPOSED
  What time _____ arrive?

3 I don't think you should drink any more coffee.
  BETTER
  You _____ any more coffee.

4 You shouldn't be so impatient.
  OUGHT
  You _____ patience.

5 I'm not allowed to stay out later than 10 o'clock.
  LET
  My parents _____ out later than 10 o'clock.

6 I always used to have to tidy my room on Saturday morning.
  MAKE
  My parents always _____ my room on Saturday morning.

7 The science teacher made me clean all the test tubes.
  MADE
  I _____ all the test tubes by the science teacher.

38

Word formation

For questions **1–14**, read the text below. Use the word given in capitals at the end of some of the lines to form a word that fits in the gap **in the same line**. There is an example at the beginning **(0)**.

Don't forget!

You may need to use the negative form of an adjective or adverb.

A driving instructor

Susan Bird, 57, is a driving **(0)** ___instructor___ in South London. **INSTRUCT**
'I was working as a shop **(1)** ___assistant___ and I realized I **ASSIST**
wanted to do something more **(2)** ___exciting___ . I saw an **EXCITE**
(3) ___advertisement___ in the newspaper and I decided to apply. **ADVERTISE**
That was over 20 years ago.
You certainly need to have a great deal of **(4)** _____ **PATIENT**
to do this job, as well as the **(5)** ___ability___ to repeat **ABLE**
things several times without getting **(6)** _____ . **ANNOY**
Although they are sometimes accused of being bad drivers,
women tend to drive more **(7)** ___carefully___ than men and **CARE**
they don't mind **(8)** ___being___ told what to do. Men, on **BE**
the other hand, usually have more **(9)** ___confidence___ , but they **CONFIDENT**
aren't very good listeners. Generally speaking, other drivers
understand what it's like to be a **(10)** ___learner___ and are **LEARN**
very considerate. **(11)** _____ , however, some can be **UNFORTUNATE**
rather **(12)** _____ ; I have been shouted at and insulted **TOLERATE**
by **(13)** ___angry___ drivers who haven't been able to **ANGER**
overtake. It's an extremely **(14)** _____ job, though, **SATISFY**
particularly when your students pass!'

Open cloze

Complete each of the following gaps with **one** word. There is an example at the beginning **(0)**.

A new life

Throughout **(0)** ___the___ 1990s I worked **(1)** ___as___ an accountant in a large furniture factory in London. I had a responsible job and was earning **(2)** _____ good living. Unfortunately, the company wasn't doing so well, and in 1999 I was **(3)** _____ redundant.
My husband and I **(4)** _____ always wanted to run **(5)** _____ own business, and we both felt that now was a good time to **(6)** _____ a risk and do something different. Jonathan, my husband, gave **(7)** _____ his well-paid but stressful job in the City and we bought a pub in a village near York.
It took **(8)** _____ both quite a long time to **(9)** _____ used to living in the countryside. Everything happens **(10)** _____ a much slower pace here, but the people are friendlier than in London and we couldn't imagine going back **(11)** _____ to live. We still work as hard **(12)** ___as___ we did before, but it's so much more satisfying working for yourself.

Writing

FCE Part 2

Short stories

1 Read the answer to the following Writing Part 2 task and then answer the questions below it.

You have decided to enter a short-story competition. The competition rules say that the story must begin with the following words:

I was beginning to feel a little nervous.

Write your **story** for the competition in **120–180** words.

> I was beginning to feel a little nervous. It was my first day at work.
>
> I said I could speak French but I couldn't. I hoped they wouldn't
>
> know that I couldn't. Everything went well. My boss was nice and
>
> he told me what I had to do. He introduced me to the other people.
>
> They were all very nice. I sat down at my desk and the phone rang.
>
> I took the phone and I started to panic. A woman was speaking
>
> to me in French and I couldn't understand her. The boss saw me.
>
> He took the phone from me. He spoke to the woman in English and
>
> then he started laughing. He told me it was his mother. She went to
>
> the dentist's and couldn't speak very well. She spoke to me in English
>
> not French!

Which of the following does the answer contain? Write Yes or No for each one.

a a variety of past tenses   _____
b a wide range of vocabulary   _____
c a selection of linking words   _____
d logical paragraphs   _____

2 Rewrite each of these four paragraphs following the instructions.

Paragraph 1

I was beginning to feel a little nervous. It was my first day **(1) at work**. I **(2) said** that I could speak French but **(3) I couldn't**. I hoped they wouldn't **(4) know** that I **(5) couldn't**.

Paragraph 2

Everything went well. My boss was very **(6) nice** and he **(7) told** me what I had to do. He introduced me to **(8) the other people**. They were all very **(9) nice**. I sat down at my desk and the phone rang.

Paragraph 3

I **(10) took the phone** and I started to panic. A woman was speaking to me in French and I couldn't understand **(11) her**. The boss saw **(12) me**. He took the phone from me.

Paragraph 4

He **(13) spoke to** the woman in English and then he **(14) started** laughing. He told me it was his mother. She **(15) went** to the dentist's and **(16) couldn't speak very well**. She **(17) spoke** to me in English not French!

Paragraph 1

Replace the words in **bold (1–5)** with a phrase from the box.

find out   had been lying   it wasn't true
as the personal assistant to a company director
had claimed at the interview

Paragraph 2

Replace the words and expressions in **bold (6–9)** with those given in box **a**:

a

friendly	explained to
helpful	my colleagues

and add the following linking words from box **b**, making any other changes which are necessary.

b

who	just as
at first	then

Paragraph 3

Replace the words and expressions in **bold (10–12)** with those given in box **a**:

a

a word she was saying	how upset I was
picked up the receiver	

and add the following linking words from box **b**, making any other changes which are necessary.

b

naturally	as soon as	when

Paragraph 4

Replace the words and expressions in **bold (13–17)** with those given in box **a**:

a

had just been to	burst out	answered
was having difficulty speaking properly		
had been talking		

and add the following linking words from box **b**, making any other changes which are necessary.

b

afterwards	to my surprise

3 Answer Yes or No again for the four questions in exercise 1, but this time about the paragraphs you have written.

4 Now write your own short story beginning with the same words.

Remember to include:
- a variety of past tenses
- a good range of vocabulary
- a selection of linking words
- logical paragraphs.

Don't forget!

Don't forget to include the words in the question!

6 Relative relationships

Reading

FCE Part 2

Gapped text

1 You are going to read an article about a family. Seven sentences have been removed from the article. Choose from the sentences **A–H** the one which fits each gap (**1–7**). There is one extra sentence which you do not need to use.

KEEPING IT IN THE FAMILY

For many people, the idea of being permanently surrounded by all their relatives may not sound like a very attractive arrangement. The occasional visit of an aunt and uncle, or a large family celebration at Christmas might be more acceptable. But the Waters family is such a close-knit one that all its members live in a row of cottages next door to each other.

The inhabitants of numbers 1–9 Bell Lane in the tiny Oxfordshire village of Cassington are all related. **1** The houses even have interconnecting gates to allow easy access. 'We're constantly going in and out of each others' houses,' says Ian Waters, grandfather of the family.

If there's a problem of any kind, help is always close at hand. 'If there's an accident or the freezer breaks down, you know you can depend on your neighbours to get you out of trouble,' says Ian. **2**

Ian Waters' family extends over three generations: the youngest is Samuel, the son of his wife's second cousin, aged 18 months; the oldest, Fred Watson, a cousin, is 99. **3** Ian and his parents moved into the street 70 years ago, when Ian was just a small boy. Ian's father, James, who wanted to supplement his income as a farmer, decided to invest in property. When other cottages in the street became available, he bought them.

Sylvia, Ian's wife, lived with her parents in a cottage just along the terrace from James Waters and his family. She first became interested in Ian when he offered to walk home with her one night after a dance. When they eventually got married in 1948, Ian's father gave the couple one of the cottages. **4** And that meant that three of the nine houses were already occupied by the same family.

This photo shows the family in 1995.

After that, other members of the family gradually came to live in the houses and by 1990 the Waters family occupied every house on the row. Cousins, brothers, sisters, nieces and daughters had all moved in. One of the last to join them was daughter, Yvonne, together with husband David and their children aged five and two. **5** But Yvonne is convinced it was worth it. 'We have the perfect babysitting arrangement,' she says. 'If we want to go out, Mum and Dad don't have far to come. And if they can't make it, someone else always can.'

6 'Mum and I do sometimes have a row,' she admits, 'but never anything too serious. And if we do fall out, it's never for very long.'

Like Yvonne, Ian feels that there are far more benefits than drawbacks. **7** 'In my lifetime there has not been a single divorce or break-up in the family. Sylvia and I have already celebrated our golden wedding anniversary, and we're certain there'll be many more such celebrations in Bell Lane in the years to come.'

A Most newly-weds at that time had to live with their parents, so they were delighted to have their own place.

B And with more than 20 members of the same family in the same street, that's a lot of neighbours who are willing to lend a hand.

C In particular, he believes that having one's relatives living nearby can help strengthen a marriage.

D They consider this lack of privacy to be the main disadvantage of living in the same street.

E They had to wait two years before a cottage became available.

F But how did they all come to be in the same row of houses?

G This means that the local driving instructor, car mechanic, plumber and doctor's receptionist all live side by side with their nearest and dearest.

H Inevitably, however, there are tensions, as with any family.

2   How many words can you find in the text for different family members? Write the words in the table below.

Words for male relatives	Words for female relatives	Words for both male and female relatives
eg _nephew_	eg _sister-in-law_	eg _grandparent_

3   Homographs are words which have the same spelling but different meanings. They may also be pronounced in different ways. Here is an example from the text:

... _all its members live in a **row** of cottages ..._   /rəʊ/ = line

'Mum and I do sometimes have a **row**.'   /raʊ/ = argument

In **1–8** below, complete the spaces in **b** with a homograph of the word you need from **a**. Decide if the two words have the same pronunciation or not and tick the appropriate box.

	Pronunciation Same	Different

Example:

a If there's a problem of any kind, help is always close at hand.
b He's such a _kind_ person; he'll do anything to help you.   ✓

1 a If there's a problem of any kind, help is always close at hand.
  b Could you _____ the window? It's a bit cold in here.

2 a Yvonne and her family came to live in Bell Lane, too.
  b Shall we go somewhere else? It's _____ crowded here.

3 a Most newly-weds at that time had to live with their parents.
  b I once went to see U2 play live _____ in concert.

4 a I'm sorry, but I don't really understand what you mean.
  b I don't think he's generous. On the contrary, he's very
  _____ .

5 a There were two football matches on television last night!
  b I can't light the fire; I haven't got any _____ .

6 a When I was a boy, I used to go fishing with my uncle.
  b I didn't have a pen, so I _____ a pencil instead.

7 a I've just read a fascinating book about identical twins.
  b The restaurant gets busy, so you'll need to _____ a table.

8 a The big wheel is the only ride I'll go on at the fair.
  b She's got lovely long _____ hair.

Vocabulary

Wordlist on page 204 of the Coursebook

A Adjectives of personality

Match each of the adjectives to an appropriate description.

| reserved | clumsy | fussy | dull | affectionate | ambitious | bossy | stubborn |

1 She worries too much about detail. _____fussy_____
2 He's always telling people what to do. _____bossy_____
3 She keeps dropping things. _____
4 He won't change his mind. _____
5 She's a bit boring. _____
6 You never know what he's thinking or feeling. _____
7 She wants to get to the top of her profession. _____
8 He never stops kissing his girlfriend. _____

B Compound adjectives

Eyes which are the shape of almonds can be described as *almond-shaped*. A person who has very pale skin can be described as *pale-skinned*.
Both *almond-shaped* and *pale-skinned* are known as compound adjectives.
Singular forms of nouns are used, eg *finger-shaped biscuits, long-eared animals*.

What compound adjectives can be used to describe the following?

1 a man who has broad shoulders	a b_____-s_____ man
2 a woman who writes with her left hand	a l___-h_____ woman
3 a girl whose hair is fair	a f___-h_____ girl
4 a boy with a round face	a r___-f____ boy
5 earrings which are in the shape of hearts	_____ earrings
6 a girl whose eyes are brown	a _____ girl
7 hair which comes down to the shoulders	_____ hair
8 a famous actor who people know very well	a ___-known actor

C Expressions with *have*

Lexical phrase list on page 124

Complete each of the gaps with one of the words from the box. Pay particular attention to the words in **bold** when making your choices.

| difficulty | common | the strength | influence | sympathy | a go | an operation | a look |

1 She'll probably have to have _____ **on** her back.
2 Come and have _____ **at** this insect.
3 I don't think I have _____ **to lift** this table on my own.
4 I had _____ **understanding** him; he spoke very fast.
5 My older brother had a big _____ **on** me when I was growing up.
6 I've never been windsurfing, but I'd love to have _____ **at** it.
7 It's a strange relationship; they don't seem to have anything **in** _____ .
8 It's your own fault you've cut yourself; I have no _____ **for** you.

Language focus

 Grammar reference on pages 210 and 211 of the Coursebook

A Causative *have*

Write out the following sentences using the correct forms of causative *have* and the main verb. Add any other words which may be necessary.

0 I/have/coat/dry-clean/week ago.
 I had my coat dry-cleaned a week ago.

1 We/have/car/repair/yesterday.
 We

2 I want/have/photo/take.

3 She/never/have/ears/pierce/before.

4 I/have/hair/cut/5 o'clock/tomorrow.

5 They/probably/have/house/paint/next month.

6 I/always/have/my suits/make/Milan/now.

B Phrasal verbs

1 There are four types of phrasal verb.

1 Intransitive verbs Verbs not followed by a direct object.	eg *to grow up* Of course I know Portsmouth. That's where **I grew up**.
2 Transitive separable verbs The direct object can go before the particle (ie it separates the verb from the particle): or after the particle: The object pronoun can only go before the particle.	eg *to let someone down* You have **let** <u>the whole school</u> **down**. You have **let down** <u>the whole school</u>. You have **let** <u>us</u> **down**. (*not* You have let down us. ✗)
3 Transitive inseparable verbs The direct object can only go after the particle (ie it cannot separate the verb from the particle): The object pronoun can only go after the particle:	eg *to fall for someone* I **fell for** <u>Gillian</u> the moment I saw her. (*not* I fell Gillian for ✗) I **fell for** <u>her</u>. (*not* I fell her for ✗)
4 Transitive inseparable verb with two particles The same rules apply as for transitive inseparable verbs with one particle:	eg *to go out with someone* She wants to **go out with** <u>Ewan</u>. She wants to **go out with** <u>him</u>.

Deciding which type a verb is

In many dictionaries the position of *someone* (or *something*) in the infinitive will tell you if the verb is:

Separable		Inseparable
to let **someone** down (Type 2) ('someone' appears between the verb and the particle)	or	to fall for **someone** (Type 3) ('someone' appears after the particle) to go out with **someone** (Type 4)

2 The verbs in the following exercise all appear in the Phrasal verb list on pages 122 and 123.

One sentence in each of the following pairs contains a mistake which is related to the use of the phrasal verb. Rewrite the incorrect sentence to make it correct.

1 a I'm very fond of my grandmother. I've always looked her up to.
  b My boyfriend was getting too serious so I decided to split up with him.
_____

2 a I think I take my father after rather than my mother.
  b We haven't really taken to the new history teacher; he's much stricter than Mr Hollis.
_____

3 a Angela and Debbie have fallen out again; Angela borrowed Debbie's watch without asking.
  b I don't earn a great deal but I get it by.
_____

4 a I blame the parents. They haven't brought up him very well.
  b Don't wear your baseball cap like that; put it on properly.
_____

5 a We'll buy you a dog, but you must promise to look after him properly.
  b He looked so lovely in the pet shop; I fell him for immediately.
_____

6 a I've decided to take up swimming.
  b These meetings take it up too much time.
_____

C Relative clauses

Complete the gaps with appropriate relative pronouns, giving alternatives where more than one answer is possible. Add commas if they are required.

1 Mr Jones _____ has taught here for 15 years will be leaving the school at the end of term. He has accepted the post of head teacher at St Mary's, the school in _____ he began his teaching career in 1980.

2 a Yesterday I spoke to the boy _____ has just moved into the house on the corner.
  b Do you mean the one _____ mum looks like Cher?

3 a Do you know a good place _____ we could go for a bop?
  b Yes, we could go to that club _____ has just opened in Farndale Street.

4 The reason _____ we're going skiing in March is because it's much cheaper then. Obviously we'd prefer to go in January _____ the snow's better but we can't afford it.

5 The fox _____ is normally a very shy animal can often be seen in city centres. It tends to keep to residential areas _____ food is usually easy to find.

6 You're the only student _____ hasn't written a letter of application. What's more, it's the third piece of homework in a row _____ you haven't done.

7 I lost that necklace _____ I was wearing on Friday _____ made me very unpopular at home. It belonged to my eldest sister _____ boyfriend gave it to her for her birthday.

Use of English

FCE Part 1

Multiple-choice cloze

For questions **1–12**, read the text below and decide which answer (**A**, **B**, **C** or **D**) best fits each gap. There is an example at the beginning (**0**).

Home-alone fathers

The number of (**0**) __single__ fathers has increased considerably in recent years in Britain. We spoke to one such dad, Steve Baker, about how he (**1**) _____ it all. Steve, 43, has (**2**) _____ up his two teenage sons since he and his wife (**3**) _____ up two years ago.

'It's no (**4**) _____ difficult for a man than it is for a woman,' says Steve. 'It's a full-time job, whoever you are. Fortunately for me, my employers were very (**5**) _____ in the first few months and they (**6**) _____ me take time off work to get myself organized. As (**7**) _____ as the housework is concerned, I don't mind cooking, as I've always been good at that; it's the ironing I can't (**8**) _____ ! Generally speaking, the boys and I get on very well (**9**) _____ but of course, sometimes we have rows. That's when I really (**10**) _____ having someone there with me to help me out.

I have had a couple of (**11**) _____ in the last two years but they haven't worked out. That has a lot to (**12**) _____ with the fact that I put my kids before anyone else. I take fatherhood very seriously.'

0	**A** alone	**B** only	**C** single	**D** unique
1	**A** gets by	**B** copes with	**C** looks after	**D** takes care
2	**A** taken	**B** made	**C** grown	**D** brought
3	**A** divorced	**B** separated	**C** parted	**D** split
4	**A** very	**B** more	**C** much	**D** at all
5	**A** comprehensive	**B** understandable	**C** sympathetic	**D** supported
6	**A** allowed	**B** offered	**C** suggested	**D** let
7	**A** far	**B** well	**C** much	**D** soon
8	**A** support	**B** hate	**C** stand	**D** help
9	**A** each one	**B** each other	**C** one another	**D** together
10	**A** miss	**B** regret	**C** want	**D** need
11	**A** relatives	**B** relationships	**C** relations	**D** partnerships
12	**A** be	**B** do	**C** see	**D** go

FCE Part 4

Transformations

Complete the second sentence so that it has a similar meaning to the first sentence, using the word given. **Do not change the word given.** You must use between **two** and **five** words, including the word given.

1 He's too short to be a good goalkeeper.
   NOT
   He's _not enough tall to be_ a good goalkeeper.

2 I couldn't concentrate because it was too noisy.
   TOO
   I couldn't concentrate because _there was too much_ noise.

3 Someone broke into our house last night.
   HAD
   We _had_ _____ last night.

4 I want them to dye my hair red at the hairdresser's.
   HAVE
   I want _my hair dyed_ red at the hairdresser's.

5 I have a great deal of respect for Susie, so I asked her.
   WHOM
   I asked Susie, _____ a great deal of respect.

6 I rescued the woman's cat but she never thanked me.
   RESCUED
   The woman _whose cat I rescued_ never thanked me.

7 The person I most admire is my grandfather.
   LOOK
   The person I most _look up to_ is my grandfather.

8 His parents said he was a disappointment to them and expected his behaviour to improve.
   DOWN
   His parents said he had _let them down_ and they expected his behaviour to improve.

Writing

FCE Part 2

Letter of application

1 Read the following Writing Part 2 task.

   You have just read this advertisement.

   Write your **letter of application** to Mrs Adams. Say why you think you would be suitable for the job and ask for more details about what you would be expected to do.
   Do not write any addresses.

2 The sentences on page 49 are from a letter which was written in reply to the advertisement in 1. Put them in the correct order and arrange them into paragraphs, according to the following paragraph plan.

   1 Reason for writing _____

   2 Personal details and qualities _____

   3 Experience _____

   4 Questions _____

   5 Closing comments _____

Summer holiday job opportunity

I am looking for a friendly young person for July and August to help look after my elderly mother while I go out to work during the day. As well as caring for my mother, you would be expected to perform light duties and do some cooking.

Personal qualities are just as important as experience. Reasonable knowledge of English essential.

Please write to Mrs Adams enclosing a reference.

Dear Mrs Adams

4 a As well as being honest and reliable, I am always cheerful and can keep smiling in any situation.

2 b I am 16 years old and I go to school in Vilnius, the capital of Lithuania.

8 c You mention in the advertisement that I would have to carry out 'light duties'.

5 d I also have a great deal of patience, particularly when dealing with other people.

10 e I enclose a reference from my English teacher, who gives details of my level of English. I look forward to receiving your reply.

3 f I know I would enjoy helping your mother and I feel I have the necessary qualities for this job.

1 g I am writing to apply for the job you advertised in last month's issue of *Jobs UK*.

6 h Apart from my personal qualities, I have experience of looking after my own grandmother, who lives here at home with us.

9 i I would be grateful if you could tell me what these duties include, and how many meals a day I would have to cook.

7 j I help to wash her, go out for short walks with her and occasionally read to her.

Yours sincerely

Dalia Vaivadaite

3 Ending the letter

Underline the appropriate alternative in each sentence:

a When we give the name of the person we are writing to at the beginning of the letter (eg 'Dear Mrs Adams'), we put 'Yours *faithfully/sincerely*' at the end.

b When we write 'Dear Sir or Madam' at the beginning of the letter, we put 'Yours *faithfully/sincerely*' at the end.

4 Write an answer to the following Writing Part 2 task, using the paragraph plan and accompanying comments and questions to help you. You should write between **120–180** words.

Before you write

Read the information about Letters of application on pages 62 and 63 in Unit 5 of the Coursebook.

You have just seen the following advertisement in an English newspaper.

We are looking for a lively young person to help look after our two children (aged eight and six) during the summer holidays. Applicants should enjoy being with children and be capable of keeping them occupied and entertained both inside and outside of the house. Reasonable command of English required. Please write to Mr and Mrs Jackson enclosing a recent photograph of yourself.

Write your **letter of application**.

Paragraph plan

1 Reason for writing

In which issue of which newspaper did you see the advertisement?

2 Personal details and qualities

- Mention your age, say what you do and give your level of English.
- Why are you interested in the job?
- What qualities do you have which might be appropriate? Select three or four adjectives from the Wordlist (Unit 6) on page 204 of the Coursebook.

3 Experience and relevant interests and skills

- What experience do you have of being with children?
- What interests and skills do you have which might be useful for this job?

Remember, you can invent information!

4 Closing comments

- What have you been asked to enclose?
- End in an appropriate way. Will you write *Yours sincerely* or *Yours faithfully*?

Reading

Multiple matching

1 You are going to read a magazine article in which four people are interviewed. For questions **1–15**, choose from the people **(A–D)**. The people may be chosen more than once. When more than one answer is required, these may be given in any order.

Before you write

Look again at the 'How to go about it' box on page 66 in Unit 6 of the Coursebook.

Which of the people state the following?

I have made unsuccessful complaints.	**1**		
I get on very well with the people below.	**2**		
I lived in the flat before I owned it.	**3**		
I don't very often have problems from noisy customers.	**4**		
I live in a busy area.	**5**		**6**
The character of the area has changed for the worse.	**7**		
The owner of the business took action to reduce the noise.	**8**		**9**
I used to have perfect working conditions.	**10**		
My sleep was often interrupted.	**11**		
I like the noise that normally comes from below.	**12**	**13**	
I intend to go and live somewhere else.	**14**	**15**	

'Just going downstairs to buy some cheese'

Living above a shop may be handy if you need something in a hurry, but it can also be a risky business. **Lynn Haywood** spoke to four people with a story to tell.

A **Masie Stigwall** I bought my flat in Chelsea with the money I made as a stunt woman in a Bond film. I've been here since the 1960s when I rented it from the friend of a friend. By the 70s I'd fallen in love with it and just had to have it for myself. It's in the King's Road, a bustling shopping street with fantastic amenities literally on the doorstep. I live above a supermarket, which was a nuisance at first; I was regularly woken up by people stacking shelves at night, and then, of course, there were the early morning deliveries. However, the owners were very reasonable when I complained and they sound-proofed the ceiling, which helped cut down the noise.

B **Paul Burton** When I first moved here I had the peace and quiet I needed to write the novel I was working on. The shop below sold wool and knitting accessories and there was a butcher's, a baker's and one or two other specialist shops in the street. They've all gone now, unfortunately; they couldn't compete with the out-of-town shopping malls and supermarkets which were springing up everywhere. The wool shop turned into a hairdresser's and now you wouldn't believe what I have to put up with. If it isn't loud music, it's the television at full volume, and then there's everyone shouting above the noise of the hairdryers. I've had words with them on more than one occasion, but they just ignore me.

C **Judie Marland** Everyone thinks that living above a pub must be a nightmare. I've been lucky, though; the landlord of the pub is very considerate and, apart from the occasional drunk singing outside at midnight, so are the people who drink there. A few years ago the landlord and I came to an agreement that he wouldn't play music above a certain volume after 10 o'clock. After a while he decided to cut out music altogether, and all I hear now is a gentle hum of conversation coming up through the floor, which I find very relaxing. I'll be sad to leave the place, but I've got my eye on a large detached house in a village near here. It's the space I need.

D **Arthur Short** It's the smell which has forced us to put our flat up for sale. Fish and chip shops are, by their nature, very smelly and there is no way we or the owner can do anything about it, so there's no point complaining. In fact, I'm on first-name terms with everyone down there and I often pop in to say hello. The noise isn't a problem; this is a lively part of town and we've always preferred places where we can hear people coming and going. We wouldn't have it any other way. We're moving out because we're tired of friends holding their nose every time they speak to us. It's getting beyond a joke now.

2 Match each phrasal verb (1–6) to its meaning (a–f) as it is used in the text. The letter in brackets indicates the paragraph in which the phrasal verb appears.

1 cut down (A)	a stop (playing/doing/eating etc)
2 spring up (B)	b tolerate
3 turn into (B)	c stop living in a house/flat
4 put up with (B)	d reduce
5 cut out (C)	e become (something different)
6 move out (D)	f appear suddenly

3 Complete each of the gaps with the correct form of an appropriate phrasal verb from exercise 2.

1 There were clear blue skies at first, but then it _____ a really horrible day.
2 It's so noisy here; I don't know how you _____ it.
3 They had a big row, after which Jim _____ and went to live with his mother.
4 A few years ago no one here knew what a cybercafe was; now they're _____ all over the city.
5 The doctor says he should _____ on the amount of whisky he drinks, but he doesn't have to _____ alcohol altogether.

4 Find expressions in the texts which have the following meanings. The letters in brackets refer to the relevant paragraphs.

1 I've complained to them (B) _____
2 made a decision together (C) _____
3 I'm interested in buying (C) _____
4 advertise that we want to sell (D) _____
5 I'm friendly with (D) _____
6 it's becoming irritating (D) _____

Vocabulary

Wordlist on page 204 of the Coursebook

A Wordsearch

Find 14 words related to shopping in the wordsearch and write them in the spaces given below. There are seven shopkeepers and seven things you find in a shop or a supermarket. The words go forwards or backwards, up or down, or diagonally.

T	T	T	S	I	R	O	L	F	G
F	R	T	I	I	E	A	E	R	C
R	O	N	G	L	L	A	O	G	H
E	L	E	O	F	L	C	E	R	E
T	L	G	O	I	E	H	L	E	C
N	E	A	D	R	W	E	S	H	K
U	Y	S	S	S	E	C	I	C	O
O	H	W	A	H	J	K	A	T	U
C	H	E	M	I	S	T	A	U	T
C	N	N	I	A	G	R	A	B	T

1 baker
2 butcher
3 chemist
4 florist
5 grocer
6 jeweller
7 newsagent

8 aisle
9 bargain
10 checkout
11 counter
12 goods
13 till
14 trolley

shopkeepers

things in shop or supermarket

51

B Multiple choice

In sentences **1–10** decide which answer, **A**, **B**, **C** or **D**, best fits each gap.

1 If you decide you don't like it, bring it back and we'll give you a _____ .
   A receipt   **B** refund   **C** guarantee   **D** reward

2 I'm sorry, we don't have any in stock at the moment, but they are on _____ .
   A request   **B** demand   **C** order   **D** ask

3 Have you been to the new shopping centre on the _____ of town?
   A centre   **B** middle   **C** outskirts   **D** suburbs

4 They didn't have any _____ peas; only tinned or frozen.
   A fresh   **B** convenient   **C** new   **D** recent

5 If it's not working, take it back to the shop. They have to replace _____ goods by law.
   A mistaken   **B** faulty   **C** lazy   **D** incorrect

6 Do you like my new dress? I bought it in the January _____ .
   A offers   **B** reductions   **C** bargains   **D** sales

7 I only got the cheese because it was on _____ ; it was £5 a kilo instead of £7.
   A offer   **B** reduction   **C** bargain   **D** sales

8 It says £5.60 on the label. You've _____ me £6.50.
   A taken   **B** deducted   **C** reduced   **D** charged

9 I have to buy Doggy Chunks for Fifi; she won't eat any other _____ of dog food.
   A selection   **B** brand   **C** mark   **D** variation

10 This car was the most expensive purchase I've ever _____ .
   A made   **B** taken   **C** put   **D** done

C Phrasal verbs with *come*

Phrasal verb list on page 122

Complete the gaps with an appropriate particle.

1 John's just phoned to say he can't come tonight; he's come _____ with a bad cold.
2 If you come _____ my red pen when you're tidying up, could you let me have it?
3 I was talking to the boss this morning and the subject of my promotion came _____ in the conversation.
4 My mum said she'd come _____ with a brilliant idea for saving money; then she said she was going to reduce my pocket money!
5 Some friends of ours came _____ last night and we watched the basketball on telly.

D Expressions with *come*

Lexical phrase list on page 124

Replace the underlined part in each sentence below with an expression from the box which has the same meaning.

| come to terms with | come on | come into fashion |
| come in handy | come true | come to |

1 We've just bought my gran a mobile phone. It might <u>be useful</u> if she has an accident or something.
2 'Oh, <u>hurry up</u>, Sandra. We're going to be late!'
3 I never thought flared trousers would <u>become popular</u> again.
4 After the injury he found it difficult to <u>accept and deal with</u> the fact that he would never again play football professionally.
5 Winning the lottery was like a dream <u>which had become a reality</u> for us.
6 'I bought a blouse, a skirt and a pair of shoes.'
   'How much did that <u>cost</u> altogether?'

E Word formation: Nouns

Noun forms for the following verbs can be found in the reading text on page 84 in Unit 7 of the Coursebook. Fill in the table and then complete the gaps in the exercise below with words from the table.

Verb	Noun	Verb	Noun
1 try	_fral_	**6** announce	_announcement_
2 cure	_cure_fure_	**7** behave	_behaviour_
3 like	_liking_	**8** create	_creation_
4 split	_split_	**9** assist	_assistance_
5 consult	_consultation_	**10** appear	_appearance_

a He has a _____ for good whisky, and he makes special trips to Scotland to buy it.

b I'd like to make a little _____ ; Shelley and I have decided to get married.

c I have a six-month _____ period and if they like the way I work, they'll give me a permanent contract.

d Her parents are worried about her _____ at school. She's always getting into trouble.

e The opening of a new car factory in Oxford has led to the _____ of 2,000 new jobs.

Language focus

 Grammar reference on pages 211 and 212 of the Coursebook

A Contrasting ideas

Choose the most appropriate sentence endings. Sometimes more than one answer is possible.

1 I'm not keen on shopping for clothes, whereas
   A my brother isn't either.
   B my sister loves it.
   C I'm not fond of shopping for food.

2 I often had rows with my brother.
   A However, we sometimes fell out.
   B However, we always remained good friends.
   C However, we never hit each other.

3 I enjoy living in the town centre, despite
   A the noise.
   B it's so noisy.
   C being so noisy.

4 Although we arrived late for the concert,
   A we missed the first few songs.
   B they wouldn't let us go in.
   C we managed to get a good seat.

5 We got on well when we shared a flat, in spite
   A of the difference in our ages.
   B of her being much older than me.
   C the fact I was much younger than her.

6 I'm glad I went to the sales, despite
   A the long wait in the cold.
   B of the fact the queue was so long.
   C having to wait so long in the cold.

B The present perfect and past simple

For questions **1–15**, complete the gaps with the present perfect or past simple form of the verbs in brackets.

How things change!

The Office for National Statistics **(1)** _____ (just/publish) a book which records how life in Britain **(2)** _____ (change) since the beginning of the 20th century.

Over the last 100 years or so, life expectancy **(3)** _____ (increase) dramatically. In 1901 men generally **(4)** _____ (expect) to live to 45, while women **(5)** _____ (live) four years longer. Since then the figure **(6)** _____ (rise) to 74 and 79 respectively and the number of people aged over 50 **(7)** _____ (double) from one sixth to one third of the population.

There **(8)** _____ (be) changes, too, in the types of illness that people suffer from. Smallpox and diphtheria **(9)** _____ (disappear) in Britain many years ago whereas cancer, AIDS and heart disease are now predominant. In the last 30 years the nation **(10)** _____ (become) wealthier: in the early 1970s the average weekly wage **(11)** _____ (be) £160; now it is twice that figure at over £340. One of the most significant changes **(12)** _____ (take) place in the area of car ownership. The motor car **(13)** _____ (have) its first test in Britain in 1896; by 1950 there **(14)** _____ (be) two million cars on the roads, and in 1998 this figure **(15)** _____ (stand) at 22 million.

C Correcting mistakes

Find the mistakes in the following sentences and rewrite them so that they are correct.

1 My father's been worked as a shop assistant for over 15 years.

_____

2 I've been breaking my leg three times in the last few years.

_____

3 Charlie Chaplin has been one of the greatest comic actors of the silent movies.

_____

4 Do you realize how long time I've been waiting here for you?

_____

5 This is the first time I see this film.

_____

6 James and I have known each other since many years.

_____

7 It's over two years since I play football.

_____

8 I cleaned three rooms of the house so far today; I'll do the other two this afternoon.

_____

Use of English

FCE Part 4

Transformations

Complete the second sentence so that it has a similar meaning to the first sentence, using the word given. **Do not change the word given**. You must use between **two** and **five** words, including the word given. There is an example at the beginning (**0**).

0 I wasn't surprised to hear that he'd failed.
   NO
   It came _____ *as no surprise* _____ to me to hear that he'd failed.

1 They haven't decided whether to sack him or not.
   COME
   They haven't _____ come up _____ about whether to sack him or not.

2 Peter has gone on a sailing course in spite of being unable to swim.
   ALTHOUGH
   Peter has gone on a sailing course _____ although he _____ to swim.

3 Although the train was late, we managed to get there on time.
   DESPITE
   We managed to get there on time, _____ late.

4 I'd rather walk than catch a bus.
   RATHER
   I'd prefer _____ to walk rather than _____ a bus.

5 I'd prefer to leave later if you don't mind.
   YET
   I'd rather _____ if you don't mind.

6 He started to learn French six years ago.
   LEARNING
   He _____ has been learning French for _____ six years.

7 We haven't seen each other for ten years.
   LAST
   The _____ last time we saw _____ each other was ten years ago.

8 I had my last hair cut two months ago.
   SINCE
   It's two months _____ since I last had _____ my hair cut.

FCE Part 3

Word formation

Use the word given in capitals at the end of some of the lines to form a word that fits in the gap **in the same line**. There is an example at the beginning (**0**).

Village life

In 1997, tired of the noise and (**0**) _pollution_ of the city, best-selling **POLLUTE**

author Will Smith and his family moved out to Chersey, a

(**1**) _picturesque_ village in the Suffolk countryside, with 53 **PICTURE**

(**2**) _inhabitants_ and one shop. Three years later they sold their **INHABIT**

(**3**) _beautiful_ 16th century cottage and moved back to London, **BEAUTY**

where they now live in a smart new (**4**) _neighbourhood_ on the outskirts **NEIGHBOUR**

of the city. So what happened? 'Chersey seemed an idyllic place

to live,' explains Will, 'a quiet, (**5**) _peaceful_ old village in extremely **PEACE**

(**6**) _pleasant_ surroundings. However, we soon became aware of **PLEASE**

the (**7**) _disadvantages_ of village life. With so little to do in Chersey, and **ADVANTAGE**

because the buses were so (**8**) _unfrequent_, our teenage children **FREQUENT**

became (**9**) _dependent_ on us to take them everywhere in the car. **DEPEND**

As for our own social life, the neighbours were rather cold and

(**10**) _unfriendly_, so we felt very isolated and lonely. It was not **FRIEND**

the rural idyll we had expected.'

FCE Part 2

Open cloze

Complete each of the following gaps with **one** word. There is an example at the beginning **(0)**.

Online shopping

Online shopping is **(0)** _____one_____ of the fastest growing areas of the Net, offering users **(1)** _____ large number of advantages over conventional shopping. Customers have access **(2)** ____to____ a wider range of goods **(3)** _____ in any shopping centre; there are no queues or parking problems; 'shops' are open 24 hours **(4)** __every__ day and purchases **(5)** _____ delivered to your door. What's **(6)** _____ , prices are competitive, and online price comparison services enable you to find the best bargains. These sites search the Net **(7)** _____ a product and then show you **(8)** _____ much different online stores are charging.

Once you have decided **(9)** __what__ you are going to buy, and who you are going to buy it from, simply click on the 'add to shopping basket' icon. **(10)** _____ you change your mind later and decide **(11)** __not__ to make the purchase, you can always cancel your order. Select the 'proceed to checkout' icon when you have everything you want, give your payment details and wait for delivery,
(12) _____ may take only a few days.

Writing

FCE Part 2

Review

Read the following Writing Part 2 instructions.

You have seen this notice in an English-language magazine.

Reviews needed!

Is there are a website you particularly like using? If so, could you write us a review of it? Tell us what you use it for and why you like it, and mention anything you don't find quite so useful. We'd also like to know who you'd recommend the site to.

The best reviews will be published next month.

Write your review for the magazine in **120–180** words.

A Structure

Read the model answer and match each of the summaries **a–d** to one of the paragraphs.

a Useful features
b Recommendation
c Features the writer does not find useful
d The website and reasons for using it

I love reading and listening to music and if I can't find what I'm looking for locally, I normally buy it from Amazon. The prices are always extremely competitive and the service is fast and efficient: sometimes a book or CD can arrive within a few days of ordering it.

What I find particularly useful about the website are the customer reviews, which are usually very informative. There are often several of these for one book or CD, so you get a fairly good idea of what something is like. I also like the fact that Amazon send you recommendations of what to buy next, based on the books or music you have already ordered.

They sell a range of other items too, including cameras, domestic appliances and sports equipment. Personally, I prefer going to shops for those kinds of things, but friends of mine use the site to buy clothes or electronic goods.

I'd recommend the site to anyone who shares my interests. It's especially handy if, like me, you live in a rural area and can't get into town very often.

B   Language analysis

a   Read the model again and answer the following questions.

Which adjectives are used to describe the positive features?
eg *competitive*

Which words are used to modify adjectives?
eg *extremely (competitive)*

Which adverbs of frequency are used?
eg *normally*

b   Complete the gaps in these sentences from the model.

1   What I find particularly useful _____ the website are the customer reviews.

2   I also like the _____ that Amazon send you recommendations.

3   _____ , I prefer going to the shops for those kinds of things.

4   I'd recommend the site to _____ who shares my interests.

C   Planning your review

Now plan your own review, following these steps:

1   Decide which website you are going to write about.
Choose one you know reasonably well and make notes under the following headings:

What I use it for
Why I like it
Features I don't find useful
Who I would recommend it to

2   Decide on a few adjectives you could use to describe the positive features.

3   Write your **review.** Follow the paragraph plan in **A** and include relevant language from **B**.

Reading

Multiple choice

1 You are going to read an article about a cruise to Australia. For questions **1–8**, choose the answer (**A**, **B**, **C** or **D**) which you think fits best according to the text.

Destination Australia

Forget long-distance flights and take the boat if you want to arrive in Australia full of energy. You might even enjoy the holiday of a lifetime on the way, says Jan Etherington.

My son, Tom, made the announcement on New Year's Eve. 'Fran and I are getting married … ' Hurrah! ' … in Australia.' Now, I've always wanted to go to Australia but like most people, I'm **put off** by the flight and the thought of arriving pale, exhausted and needing a week to recover. Even with a stopover, you face two long-distance flights. But it doesn't have to be like that. I found a way to arrive suntanned, refreshed, and ready for action. I went by boat, on the Saga Rose world cruise.

If I'd had the time and money, I could have gone all the way round the world, but the great thing about this cruise is that you can embark and disembark wherever you wish. If you want to get to Australia or New Zealand, take a shorter flight somewhere, join the world cruise and arrive in civilized style. I **picked** it **up** in Valparaiso (the port for Santiago, Chile) and sailed on from there to Sydney.

The Saga Rose is a good-looking ship. Launched in 1965, she is highly regarded by maritime experts for her elegant lines. Passenger capacity is 587, but we were fewer than 400, with 350, largely Filipino, crew who were smart, efficient and full of good humour. It was the cleanest ship I'd ever seen and the variety and freshness of the meals was impressive, with a welcome freedom to dine in the evening at any time between 7.15 and 9pm.

I met lots of accomplished, funny, clever, attractive people on the ship. Good company and a well-run ship are important, because, on this stretch of the journey, we were together for a month – long enough to learn a skill. I **took up** salsa, inspired by dance teacher, Thabo, who made us believe we were good enough to perform in front of passengers and crew.

Julia's jewellery-making classes were surprisingly popular. Even cynics (like me) were impressed as, using seeds and beads from local sources, students produced desirable costume jewellery. And the watercolour classes gave amateurs the tools to capture the passing scenes more imaginatively than with a digital camera. There were also lectures and talks, from ex-MPs and diplomats, plus standing-room only presentations by Hilary Kay and Christopher Lewis, from the popular television programme *The Antiques Roadshow*. *line 46*

Each day brought a once-in-a-lifetime experience. From Santiago, we sailed west, across the South Pacific. As we neared each island, usually at dawn, peering sleepily through binoculars, the dot on the horizon would slowly form a personality. There were no two alike. Easter Island was soft, undulating, like a huge, warm, green pillow. But the knowledge that the islanders had **used up** their resources and destroyed their environment, by their obsessive building of the giant Moai statues, lent it a terrible sadness and mystery. Tahiti looks as if it needs ironing. The volcanic hills are jagged and sharp. Lush and green, it is full of waterfalls and wild forests. A dramatic place, it seems conscious of its role as the most important island in French Polynesia. *line 59*

Each Pacific island is a long way from its neighbour, which meant many 'sea days'. These proved a lovely way to **catch up on** reading and while away hours scanning the horizon, where every wave appeared to be a whale or a dolphin. I kept fit by walking the promenade deck every morning (seven circuits is a mile), swimming in the seawater pool and forgoing puddings and cakes (I had a wedding outfit to get into).

As we cruised into Sydney at sunrise, it was like sailing into a familiar postcard. We passed the opera house, slid under the Harbour bridge and, on the quayside, Tom and Fran waved banners of welcome. I leapt off, relaxed, fit and full of energy. 'Let's go shopping for a hat!'

1 In the first paragraph we learn that the writer
   A does not like travel.
   B was not in very good health.
   C had not been to Australia before.
   D had not seen her son for a long time.

2 What according to the writer is the main advantage of the Saga Rose cruise?
   A It offers the traveller flexibility.
   B It is more affordable than flying.
   C It takes the traveller right round the world.
   D It is more comfortable than other cruises.

3 The writer says she was pleased that
   A the ship was not completely full.
   B the crew was mainly Filipino.
   C she could choose her evening mealtime.
   D she had decided to travel alone.

4 The writer says she had not expected
   A to have to spend so long on board the ship.
   B to get on so well with her fellow travellers.
   C to enjoy the organized activities so much.
   D to see such good results from one of the classes.

5 What does the writer mean by 'standing-room only presentations' in line 46?
   A there were no seats for the two presenters
   B the presentations were extremely well attended
   C a special room was provided for the presentations
   D most people in the audience had to stand

6 What does the writer say about the islands in the South Pacific?
   A She only ever saw them from a distance.
   B They were all very different from each other.
   C There were two that she did not particularly like.
   D She would not choose to return to any of them.

7 What does 'it' in line 59 refer to?
   A the knowledge of what the islanders had done
   B the destruction of the environment
   C the building of the statues
   D Easter Island

8 Whilst sailing through the South Pacific, the writer says
   A she spent a long time on board ship.
   B she saw a wide variety of marine life.
   C she was able to go swimming in the sea.
   D she ate a large amount of sweet food.

2 Match the following meanings to the highlighted phrasal verbs as they are used in the text. The meanings show the infinitive of the verbs.

   a start doing a new activity
   b spend time doing an activity you have not had time to do recently
   c make you decide not to do something
   d finish a supply of something
   e join and follow a journey or route

Vocabulary

Wordlist on page 204 of the Coursebook

Confusing words

Choose the correct alternative in each sentence **1–10**.

1 Everyone thought the holiday was great *fun/funny* but I didn't have such a good time.

2 The area near the palace gates was *full/crowded* with tourists.

3 The facilities on this *camping/campsite* are excellent.

4 Have you decided where you're going on *holiday/holidays* yet?

5 We always *stay/live* in the same hotel when we go to London.

6 All the hotels at the ski *station/resort* are fully booked, unfortunately.

7 We didn't bring back any *souvenirs/memories* from our holiday. We didn't see anything worth buying.

8 From the top of the cathedral tower there are some spectacular *sights/sites/views* of the surrounding countryside.

9 The cost of the *trip/journey/travel* includes two nights in a four-star hotel with half-board.

10 She didn't enjoy the Mediterranean *voyage/cruise/tour* at all; she was seasick most of the time.

Language focus

 Grammar reference on page 212 of the Coursebook

The future

1   Each of the underlined future forms is inappropriate. Rewrite each sentence with a more suitable future form.

1 Have you cut your finger? Come into the bathroom and <u>I put</u> a plaster on it.

_____

2 Congratulations! I hear <u>you will have</u> a baby.

_____

3 I've arranged to play tennis with Miguel tomorrow morning. <u>We're about to meet</u> at the sports centre at 10 am.

_____

4 Can you wake me up before <u>you will leave</u> for work tomorrow morning?

_____

5 I don't think <u>I'm getting</u> more than 50% in the exam; I never do well at physics.

_____

6 This time tomorrow <u>we're going to sit</u> on the plane, probably somewhere over the Alps.

_____

7 What <u>do you do</u> next weekend? Have you made any plans?

_____

8 Phone me on Friday. <u>I'm speaking</u> to Greg by then, so I can tell you what his plans are.

_____

2 Complete each of the gaps with an appropriate future form of the verb in brackets.

1 That bag looks very heavy. I __'ll carry__ (carry) it for you, if you want.

2 I _____ (have) my eyes tested on Saturday. I've got an appointment for 10.30.

3 The autumn term _____ (end) on December 23rd, the same day as my birthday. I _____ (be) 15 then.

4 No, don't phone me at 8 o'clock. I _____ (watch) the match at that time. Phone me at 9 instead; it _____ (finish) by then.

5 I _____ (get) some new clothes tomorrow; I've decided I need to change my look.

6 I think we should wait until Kevin _____ (get) back.

7 Don't forget that when they get here this evening, they _____ (travel) for over 12 hours, so I expect they _____ (want) to go straight to bed.

8 'Katie? Hi, it's Antonio. Listen, I'm on the train at Croydon, so I _____ (be) at Brighton station at five past nine. Can you pick me up?'

Use of English

FCE Part 4

Transformations: Phrasal verbs revision

Complete the second sentence so that it has a similar meaning to the first sentence, using the word given. **Do not change the word given.** You must use between **two** and **five** words, including the word given. There is an example at the beginning **(0)**.

Each of these transformations requires you to use a phrasal verb from Units 1–8.

0 I've had enough of your rudeness.
PUT
I am not going _to put up with_ your rudeness any more.

1 I just can't wait for the Christmas holidays!
LOOKING
I'm looking forward to the Christmas holidays!

2 They'll probably employ him for two months in the summer.
LIKELY
They _____ likely to take him on for two months in the summer.

3 The fact that bus travel is so cheap compensates for the lack of comfort.
MAKES
The low cost of travelling _____ for the lack of comfort.

4 I think he's on the point of starting his own company.
SET
I think he's about _____ to set up his own company.

5 Their relationship seems very good.
GET
It looks as _____ very well with each other.

6 Have you thought of a name for your dog yet?
COME
Have you _____ come up with a name for your dog yet?

7 I'm not going to smoke ever again after today.
GIVE
I've decided _____ to give up smoking from tomorrow.

8 Sue and Alan ended their relationship a long time ago.
SPLIT
Sue and Alan _____ split up with each other a long time ago.

FCE Part 2

Open cloze

For questions **1–12**, read the text below and think of the word which best fits each gap. Use only **one** word in each gap. There is an example at the beginning (**0**).

A place in the sun

Southern Spain's Costa del Sol, which stretches (**0**) _from_ Nerja in the east to Manilva in the west, is one of the most famous tourist areas (**1**) ___in___ the world. Blessed with an average of 320 days of sunshine (**2**) __every__ year, the coastline offers the perfect holiday destination for anyone wanting to switch (**3**) __off__ and unwind. As (**4**) __well__ as its beautiful sun-soaked beaches and excellent gastronomy, the region boasts no fewer (**5**) __than__ thirty golf courses, providing amateurs and professionals alike (**6**) __to__ year-round golfing opportunities. Not for nothing was the term 'Costa del Golf' coined in the late 1980s to describe the area.

Tourists looking for a more cultural experience will also (**7**) __not__ be disappointed. With its Roman theatre, Renaissance-style cathedral and Arab castle, the city of Málaga (**8**) __is__ well worth a visit. Described (**9**) __as__ the 'City of Paradise' by the Nobel prize winner for literature, Vicente Aleixandre, Málaga is a historical jewel in (**10**) __lots of__ different peoples and cultures have left their mark over the centuries. It is also the birthplace of Picasso, (**11**) __whose__ house still stands today just a short distance from the Museo Picasso, (**12**) __one__ of over twenty museums in the city.

FCE Part 3

Word formation

Use the word given in capitals at the end of some of the lines to form a word that fits in the gap **in the same line**.

1 As it grew hotter, even the managing director _____ his tie and undid his collar button. **LOOSE**

2 If we introduced another foreign language in the school, we'd have to _____ the school day. **LONG**

3 Owing to continuous heavy rain, driving conditions have _____ in the past few hours. **WORSE**

4 Don't come near me when I'm _____ the knife, dear. I don't want you to cut yourself. **SHARP**

5 Free divers are now diving to _____ of over 80 metres. **DEEP**

6 Then heat the sauce until it _____. **THICK**

7 It's thought that listening to loud music on a regular basis can eventually lead to partial _____. **DEAF**

8 His face had _____ with anger. It looked as if he might explode! **RED**

9 It was raining heavily in the morning, but by midday the weather had _____ up and we were able to go out. **BRIGHT**

10 There have been several serious accidents recently, so the police are _____ up on drunken driving. **TIGHT**

Writing

Formal letters and emails

Read the following Writing Part 1 question. You do not need to write an answer.

You have just read the entry for the town of Rington in the guidebook *Around Britain*. You know Rington very well and you feel that some improvements could be made to the entry. Read the extract from the guidebook entry and the notes you have made. Then write a letter to the publishers, using **all** your notes.

Around Britain – **Rington**

As you would expect, there are many souvenir shops in the centre of Rington, selling a wide range of gifts, including the delicious local honey and jam. There are also plenty of places to eat in the town. We recommend 'Dylan's' restaurant in Gardner Street for good English food, but be prepared for high prices. After lunch you might like to go for a walk alongside the River Bane, which flows through the town. The river will take you into open countryside, which, surprisingly, is just 15 minutes on foot from the centre. It is a shame that the water is rather polluted, but this will not ruin your enjoyment of the walk. Rington is famous for its many historic monuments, some dating from Roman times.

and also .... — local honey and jam

yes, but ... — high prices

not any more — water is rather polluted

32

Write a **letter** in **120–150** words in an appropriate style. Do not write any postal addresses.

> *Notes*
> • *Congratulations – the guidebook is very ...*
> • *Suggest how the entry could be improved*

A Model

Read this answer to the Writing question on page 63, then complete each gap with an appropriate expression from the box.

it is true	no longer the case	you claim that
it is worth	congratulate you on	
you could also perhaps mention		with regard to

Dear Sir or Madam

I would like to **(a)** _____ your excellent guidebook Around Britain. I find it very informative and well illustrated, and always take my copy with me when I travel around the country. However, I would like to suggest some improvements which I feel could be made **(b)** _____ the entry on Rington.

Firstly, you include the local honey and jam as examples of gifts one can buy here, but **(c)** _____ the handmade knives for which the area is famous. In addition, although **(d)** _____ that 'Dylan's' restaurant is not cheap, **(e)** _____ pointing out that the portions are usually very large. Finally, **(f)** _____ the River Bane is polluted, but this is **(g)** _____. It has recently been cleaned and in some places it is possible to swim.

I hope you find this information useful.

Yours faithfully

Alice Matheson

B Analysis

Answer the following questions about the model letter.

1 Which linking words are used for contrasting ideas?
2 Which linking words and expressions are used for adding to the list of points?
3 Which expressions in the letter have the following meanings?
   a in connection with
   b you're right about the fact that
   c not correct any more

C Adding relevant information

Candidates who write good answers to Part 1 questions build on the notes given by adding relevant information. What information has the writer of the model added for each of the following? The first one has been done for you.

the guidebook: _and always take my copy with me when I travel around the country._

the gifts: _____

the restaurant: _____

the river: _____

D   Writing task

Read the following Writing Part 1 question. Read section E Preparation before you write your answer.

You have just read the entry for the town of Blackingham in *The Tourist Webguide to Britain* on the Internet. You know Blackingham very well and you feel that some improvements could be made to the entry. Read the printout of the extract from the website and the notes you have made. Then write an **email** to *The Tourist Webguide,* using **all** your notes.

The Tourist Webguide to Britain – Blackingham

Visitors to Blackingham usually head straight for the historic centre, with its attractive Georgian architecture and 14th century cathedral. Unfortunately, the town is a victim of its own success and <u>traffic is a problem.</u> The narrow streets quickly fill up with cars and lorries, causing inconvenience for both shoppers and tourists.

not any more

Next to the cathedral is the splendid Blackingham Town Museum, with <u>exhibits</u> from the town's 2000-year history. After seeing the sights you might like to relax in the Botanical Gardens, where there are plenty of seats for you to rest your tired legs. The Gardens are <u>rather small,</u> so do not expect anything along the same lines as Kew Gardens in London.

include examples

yes, but ...

Page 1 **2** 3 4

| Home | Other Regions | About the Tourist Webguide | Contact us |

Notes
- *Congratulations – the website is very ...*
- *Suggest how the entry could be improved*

E   Preparation

Answer the following questions to give you some ideas about what to include in your answer:

the website: When do you make use of *The Tourist Webguide to Britain*?
the traffic: What was done to solve the traffic problem?
the museum: What examples of exhibits could be included in the entry?
the Gardens: What makes the Botanical Gardens so interesting to visit?

Write your **email** in **120–150 words**. You must use grammatically correct sentences with accurate spelling and punctuation in a style appropriate for the situation.

What to expect in the exam

- In the First Certificate exam the requirements for a formal email are similar to those for a formal letter.
- An email box will be printed at the top of the answer page.

Gapped text

1 You are going to read an article about a government report on UFOs. Seven sentences have been removed from the article. Choose from the sentences **A–H** the one which fits each gap (**1–7**). There is one extra sentence which you do not need to use.

Don't forget!

- Look for connections between the language in the text and the language in the missing sentences. To help you, key words and phrases have been underlined in the missing sentences.
- One of the sentences **A–H** is not required.

Just a load of hot air!

They **glow**, move across the sky at incredible speed and are invisible to radar. The mysterious shapes have for decades been **cited** by UFO enthusiasts as proof that we have attracted visitors from another world.

1 After four years of study they have concluded that they are not flying saucers, but 'plasmas' of gas caused by charges of electricity in the atmosphere. The study by the Defence Intelligence Staff examined 30 years of apparent flying saucer sightings, which average about 100 a year.

Their 400-page report found that most of those who reported seeing UFOs – usually as glowing round or cigar-shaped objects – were not fantasists or hoaxers playing tricks. **2** The bright plasmas are created by charges of electricity. When air **flows** into them they are transformed into aerodynamic shapes which appear to fly at incredible speeds.

The electromagnetic fields can also cause responses in the brain, **tricking** observers into thinking they are seeing even more vivid impressions, the study found. Because they are electrically charged, plasmas can change shape or colour when **struck** by another energy source – such as radio signals by UFO spotters. **3** The scientists concluded they now have 'a reasonably justified explanation' for the sightings that had previously been difficult to describe.

UFO watchers have insisted that the theory still fails to explain many sightings and the study of the gas plasmas is at any rate 'poorly understood'. Codenamed Project Condign, the secret study began in 1996, apparently without the knowledge of then defence secretary Michael Portillo. **4** The aim was to assess any military threat from sightings of unexplained flying objects, many of which appeared to '**hover**, land, take off, accelerate to exceptional velocities and vanish'.

The study was released under the Freedom of Information Act. Files previously released under this law showed that the Ministry of Defence maintained a special unit to **log** sightings of UFOs by the public and the military. **5** They described seeing 'bright objects hanging over the sea' around three miles from the coast at a height of around 5,000ft.

In July 1976, the captain of a British Airways Tri-Star on a return flight from Portugal told air traffic controllers of 'four objects – two round brilliant white, two cigar-shaped' 18 miles north of Faro. **6** A spokesman for the Ministry of Defence said: 'We have to check any report of an unidentified flying object to ensure it's not a threat. That's what this report was about. Once we are satisfied there is no threat, as this report concluded, we take no further action. We are not a UFO club.'

7 'Even physicists studying plasma clouds do not fully understand them,' she said, 'so it is ridiculous for the Government to use a little known and poorly understood phenomenon as the main explanation for most UFO sightings.' She added: 'It may **account for** some, but by no means all. It does not explain incidents where ground trace evidence of UFOs has been left behind or where there is film footage of flying objects. The MoD will never release any documents that suggest there may be some mystery surrounding UFO sightings, but the simple fact is that some are mysterious.'

A These included a report by Flight Lieutenant A M Wood and two non-commissioned officers in Northumberland in July 1977.

B 'This has led ufologists to imagine that an alien response is being given to their signals,' said the report.

C Judy Jaafar, secretary of the British UFO Research Association, criticized the report.

D Defence chiefs, however, have a rather less exciting explanation for the glowing objects in the sky.

E However, the Government seems to agree that not all incidents such as these can be explained scientifically.

F It was completed four years later under Geoff Hoon.

G Fighter planes were sent to investigate and shortly afterwards the crew on two other commercial flights in the same area reported similar sightings.

H They were describing unusual but entirely natural events in the atmosphere.

2   Match the highlighted verbs in the article with the meanings **a–h** below. The meanings are expressed as infinitives.

  a hit
  b deceive; make someone believe something which is not true
  c be the explanation or cause of something
  d produce a continuous light
  e mention (in order to support a belief)
  f record officially
  g move continuously
  h stay in the same place in the air

3   Fill each of the gaps with the appropriate form of one of the highlighted verbs in the text.

  1 Believing the email – supposedly from Boyd's Bank – to be genuine, she was _____ **into** disclosing her credit card details.

  2 Poor exam results were _____ **as evidence of** the failure of the Government's education policies.

  3 The demonstration was accompanied by two police **helicopters** _____ noisily overhead.

  4 We saw a large, burnt-out tree which had probably been _____ **by lightning**.

  5 Bad weather _____ 76% of delays at UK airports last year.

  6 They live next to a motorway, so a constant stream of **traffic** _____ past their house.

  7 She knew he was still there: she could see his **cigarette** _____ in the dark.

  8 Before itemized telephone bills we had to _____ all personal **calls** from the office in a red notebook.

Vocabulary

A Phrasal verbs

Phrasal verb list on page 122

Match each sentence beginning on the left with an appropriate ending on the right.

1 As soon as I **gave up**	**a** **state secrets**, he was arrested and held in jail.
2 The cooker was **giving off**	**b** **the homework** tomorrow morning.
3 Suspected of **giving away**	**c** **smoking**, I felt a lot better.
4 He listened closely as they **gave out**	**d** **food** to homeless people.
5 She said we had to **give in**	**e** **a strange smell,** so I got someone to look at it.
6 Street Aid is a charity which **gives out**	**f** **the money** I lent him until Friday.
7 He says he can't **give back**	**g** **the winning lottery numbers** on the news.

B Expressions with *give*

Lexical phrase list on page 124

Complete each of the gaps with one of the words in the box.

lift	example	idea	impression
call	party	hand	permission

1 'Risk' is a verb which takes the gerund. Can anyone give another _____ ?
2 Dave gave me a _____ to work in his new car this morning.
3 I can't move this table on my own. Can anyone give me a _____ ?
4 The manager has given me _____ to take two days off work.
5 He gave me the _____ that he was bored; he kept sighing during the lesson.
6 I won't be at home tomorrow, but you can give me a _____ on my mobile?
7 Would you give me some _____ of what time you'll be coming home, so I'll know when to have dinner ready for.

C Collocations

One adjective in each group is not normally used in partnership with the noun in capital letters. Underline the word which does not fit. There is an example at the beginning **(0)**.

0 deep	impatient	open-air	loud	SIGH
1 piercing	loud	blank	high-pitched	SCREAM
2 tender	big	passionate	broad	KISS
3 full	precise	nervous	relevant	DETAILS
4 lengthy	piercing	impressive	boring	SPEECH
5 deep	tender	broad	friendly	SMILE
6 loud	full	nervous	cruel	LAUGH
7 impressive	nasty	great	terrible	SHOCK

D Revision: *get*

1 It was such a sad, depressing film; it really got me _____ .
2 We all suffered from food poisoning on holiday. I'm OK now, but my mum and dad still haven't got _____ it.
3 I'm going to try to get _____ for the weekend. I'll probably go to the coast.
4 I don't know how they get _____ ; they're both unemployed and they've got three children.

Language focus

 Grammar reference on page 213 of the Coursebook

A Modal verbs of speculation

1 There is a mistake in five of the sentences in **1–10** below. Find the mistakes and rewrite the sentences to make them correct.

   1 I can't find my keys. I think I might leave them on my desk at work. *[have left]*

   2 The dog's barking a lot. He might be trying to tell us something.

   3 Sally's not answering the phone. She can have gone away for the weekend, or perhaps she's just gone to the shops. *[can]*

   4 It's his birthday tomorrow, so he must be excited.

   5 They said they'd found out what was wrong with the washing machine, but they can't have done because it's still not working properly. *[couldn't have done]*

   6 **a:** Andrea never wears that blouse we bought her. *[may/might]*

   b: Well, she might not like the colour, it may not go with her skirts or it could not be the right size. Who knows? *[couldn't go]*

   7 Jim mustn't be going out with Sue; she's just got engaged to Doug. *[can't/couldn't]*

   8 It couldn't have run out of petrol. I filled it up this morning before we left.

   9 It's a shame Mark hasn't come. He must decide to stay at home. *[have decided]*

   10 The tennis rackets aren't in the car. You must have forgotten to put them in.

2 Use modal verbs to give one or more explanations for the following situations.

   Example:
   He can't drive for two months.
   He could have broken his leg or his wife might be using the car.

   1 He looks exhausted.
   _____

   2 She isn't eating very much at the moment.
   _____

   3 There's a lot of traffic in the city centre today.
   _____

   4 The plants have all died.
   _____

   5 The police came to speak to the neighbours this morning.
   _____

   6 John seems very happy these days.
   _____

   7 Why are all those people shouting?
   _____

   8 I was sure I'd parked my car here. Where is it?
   _____

B Question tags

Complete each of the following phrases with an appropriate question tag.

1 He hasn't been here long, _____ ?
2 I'm getting old, _____ ?
3 He plays for Barcelona, _____ ?
4 You'd like to come, _____ ?
5 She said she was ill, _____ ?
6 Don't make too much noise, _____ ?
7 Help me lift this box, _____ ?
8 Let's go to the cinema, _____ ?
9 Nothing serious happened, _____ ?
10 No one lives here now, _____ ?

Use of English

FCE Part 1

Multiple-choice cloze

For questions **1–12**, read the text below and decide which answer (**A**, **B**, **C** or **D**) best fits each space. There is an example at the beginning (**0**).

The wildman of China

Most people are (**0**) _familiar_ with the yeti, a large hairy man-like creature, which is (**1**) _____ to live in the Himalayas. (**2**) _____ , you might not have heard of the 'yeren' or 'wildman' of China, which was mentioned and drawn for the first (**3**) _____ more than 2,000 years ago. In the (**4**) _____ 40 years there have been over 200 (**5**) _____ of the yeren in the Shennongjia Nature Reserve in central Hubei province.

(**6**) _____ the size of footprints which have been found, the yeren could weigh as much as 300 kilos. Those who (**7**) _____ to have seen it have described it as approximately 1.6 metres tall, with long red hair, rounded eyes and a broad forehead. It also seems (**8**) _____ of an incredible range of calls and noises. When disturbed, it is said to sound like a dog, a wolf, a donkey and (**9**) _____ a crying child.

In 1980 a Chinese scientist (**10**) _____ up in a gorilla costume and entered a forest in the (**11**) _____ of getting a closer look at a yeren. Not surprisingly he failed, as have so many others who have gone in (**12**) _____ of this elusive creature.

0	**A** aware	**B** conscious	**C** familiar	**D** known
1	**A** reported	**B** informed	**C** noticed	**D** announced
2	**A** Actually	**B** Instead	**C** However	**D** Moreover
3	**A** time	**B** event	**C** occasion	**D** moment
4	**A** latest	**B** ultimate	**C** recent	**D** last
5	**A** views	**B** visions	**C** sightings	**D** looks
6	**A** Taken	**B** Given	**C** Considered	**D** Seen
7	**A** claim	**B** state	**C** say	**D** tell
8	**A** able	**B** competent	**C** capable	**D** powerful
9	**A** just	**B** too	**C** well	**D** even
10	**A** wore	**B** dressed	**C** put	**D** changed
11	**A** attempt	**B** hope	**C** order	**D** wish
12	**A** search	**B** look	**C** hunt	**D** sight

FCE Part 3 **Word formation**

1 Write the adjectives and adverbs which are formed from the following nouns. Use the suffixes -al, -ous or -y and make any other changes which are necessary. There is an example at the beginning (**0**).

Noun	Adjective	Adverb
0 noise	*noisy*	*noisily*
1 humour	humorous	humorously
2 ambition	ambitious	ambitiously
3 benefit	beneficial	beneficially
4 hunger	hungry	hungrily
5 anxiety	anxious	anxiously
6 origin	original	originally

2 Complete the table with the correct form of the words given. There is an example at the beginning (**0**).

Verb	Noun	Adjective +	Adjective –
0 appreciate	*appreciation*	*appreciative*	*unappreciative*
1 attract	attraction	attractive	unattractive
2 decide	decision	decided	undecided
3 excite	excitement	exciting	unexciting
4	imagination		unimaginative
5	obedience		disobedient
6 offend			
7 please			
8	success		
9	thought		
10	tolerance	tolerant	intolerant

3 Complete each gap with the appropriate form of the words in capitals. If the missing word is a **noun**, you may need a plural form. If the missing word is an **adjective** or **adverb**, you may need a negative form. There is an example at the beginning (**0**).

0 He gave her a small present to show his _appreciation_ for her kindness. **APPRECIATE**

1 I think it's an extremely _____ building; it's far too big and it ruins the character of the area **ATTRACTION**

2 I'm afraid I'm not very good at making _____ . I never know what the best thing to do is. **DECIDE**

3 There was a great deal of _____ when the Queen arrived to open the new hospital. **EXCITE**

4 You really should read one of the Harry Potter books. They're very _____ written. **IMAGINATION**

5 He never does as he's told; he's so _____ . **OBEDIENCE**

6 You shouldn't take _____ . I'm sure he didn't mean what he said. **OFFEND**

7 I always have a glass of wine with my meal. It's one of my few _____ . **PLEASE**

8 78-year-old Bill Baxter has _____ completed his third London Marathon. **SUCCESS**

9 Thank you for the flowers. That was very _____ of you. **THOUGHT**

10 You have a very _____ attitude. You should try to accept other people's opinions. **TOLERANCE**

Writing

Essays

Read the following Writing Part 2 instructions.

Your class has been working on a project on traditional customs and celebrations. Now your teacher has asked you to write an essay giving your opinion on the following statement:

Traditional celebrations have no relevance in today's world and are a waste of time and money.

Write your **essay** in **120–180** words.

A Model

Read the example essay below, and then complete each of the spaces with one of the words in the box.

however	extent	think	although	argument
conclude	moreover	hand	opinion	

> Every country has its own traditions, some of which have existed for centuries. In my **(1)** _____ we should do everything possible to preserve them.
>
> Some people **(2)** _____ that in today's high-tech world traditional celebrations are too old-fashioned and irrelevant to our lives. **(3)** _____ , events such as Carnival are important, as they bring communities together and make us think about other people and not just computers.
>
> Another **(4)** _____ against traditional festivals is that they are expensive to organize. To some **(5)** _____ this is true, particularly when there are firework displays or parades. On the other **(6)** _____ , it is a small price to pay for brightening up our lives with entertainment and colour. **(7)** _____ , celebrations like the 'Fallas' in my home town of Valencia attract many tourists and their money.
>
> Finally, **(8)** _____ I agree that some traditional customs have lost their original significance, they can provide an opportunity for us to learn about our past. For example, Bonfire Night teaches British children about a particular period of their country's history.
>
> To **(9)** _____ , traditional celebrations are a source of great pleasure and interest, and they are certainly worth keeping.

Which words in the essay above are used to introduce the three examples of traditional celebrations?

B Organization

Which of these paragraph plans does the example essay follow?

A	B
1 Introduction: writer's general opinion	1 Introduction: writer's general opinion
2 First point for the statement	2 First point for the statement and writer's argument against this point.
3 Second point for the statement	3 Second point for the statement and writer's argument against this point.
4 Third point for the statement	4 Third point for the statement and writer's argument against this point.
5 Conclusion: writer states opinion	5 Conclusion: writer states opinion again

C Ideas

Read these three statements which were given to a class as essay titles.

A *Sport today has become far too competitive and is no longer enjoyable.*
B *Village life is more pleasant than city life.*
C *All students should spend a year working before they go to university.*

Match the following ideas to the appropriate statement and then say whether the students who wrote them agreed or disagreed with the statement. The first one has been done for you.

1 It's big business now – there's too much money involved. *A (agree)*
2 There's nothing to do there. It's so dull and boring.
3 You might do a job which is completely irrelevant to what you do after university.
4 People don't socialize like they do in the city.
5 Athletes never used to take drugs. Breaking world records doesn't mean anything now.
6 You'd be taking away jobs from unemployed people.
7 Violence at football matches is just one example of the way some people take it too seriously.
8 It sounds like a waste of time. I can't see how it would make me a better person.
9 It's not as quiet as you might think – all those animals waking you up every morning.
10 Employers would probably use it as a way of getting cheap labour.
11 Sport is controlled by politicians, who use it to make their country look better than others.
12 It gets busy and crowded at the weekend because everyone from the city goes there to get away from it all.

D Writing task

Now write an **essay** in **120–180** words giving your opinion on **one** of the three statements **A**, **B** or **C** in section **C** above.

How to go about it

1 Choose one of the statements and write down arguments for (in favour of) it and arguments against it. You may use the ideas in section C above.
2 Decide whether you agree or disagree with the statement, then write a paragraph plan, using plan B in section B above. Try to include examples to support your arguments.
3 Decide which linking words you are going to use. You will find more in the Coursebook in the Writing sections for Units 3 and 8.
4 Write your essay.

Reading

Multiple matching

1 You are going to read a newspaper article about techniques used by thieves. For questions **1–15**, choose from the people **(A–E)**. The people may be chosen more than once. When more than one answer is required, these may be given in any order.

A Steve Sheppardson
B Jane Sinson
C Kathryn Adams
D William Walker
E Steven Nicholls

Which of the people suggest the following?

I was shortly going to be leaving the city. `1 ☐`

I was unable to chase the thieves as they fled. `2 ☐`

I suspected something was wrong. `3 ☐` `4 ☐`

It was not as serious as it might have been. `5 ☐`

I had problems understanding them. `6 ☐`

It made me suspicious for the rest of my visit. `7 ☐`

I gave them the impression I had been taken in. `8 ☐`

I was not the first person to be tricked in this way. `9 ☐`

I did not fall for the trick. `10 ☐` `11 ☐`

My actions made it obvious I was not a local. `12 ☐`

I gave a small reward. `13 ☐`

Something which smelled bad was used to create confusion. `14 ☐`

I became aware something was wrong much later. `15 ☐`

Travellers' Tales
Hanging on to your Money

When I reported the incident of how three men recently attempted to rob me at Krakow bus station, several readers got in touch with their own stories.

Steve Sheppardson reports an experience in Manhattan: 'We were sitting on a park bench and I was carrying a large camera bag over my shoulder. When a group of teenagers ran past and around us, I held tightly on to the camera
5 thinking this might be more than just youngsters having fun.

'Five minutes later, somebody pointed to the back of my jacket and held their nose – when I took off the jacket, the back was covered in a wet, sticky substance with an unpleasant odour. At this point we got lucky – a shop
10 assistant came out, invited us in to clean up and told us what had happened: the kids we saw had squirted my back with something like washing-up liquid that sticks and makes a mess. In the confusion, many people put their bag down to take their jacket off and the bag is
15 snatched when they are least expecting it.'

A similar incident happened to **Jane Sinson** in New Delhi: 'I was standing near the Palika bazaar when two young men walked up to me. One drew attention to a mess of some kind on my sandal. They took me to a very
20 conveniently located shoe cleaner and told me it would b 150 rupees (£3) to clean the sandal.

'The young men were unaware that, although white, I speak Hindi as I have Indian relatives by marriage. I let the shoe cleaner do his work with the young men there,
25 and offered him the usual payment of 50 rupees. When they tried to protest, I spoke to them in Hindi, at which point they realized they had picked the wrong person.'

This account comes from **Kathryn Adams**: 'I was driving into Barcelona recently when the car in front stalled at th
30 lights when they went green – the driver got out and in the confusion (as I soon found out) knifed my back

2 Match each word on the left with its meaning on the right. The line numbers are given in brackets.

1 pointed (6)	**a** drew attention to something by holding out a finger
2 squirted (11)	**b** taken quickly
3 sticks (12)	**c** covered with a liquid (from a tube or similar)
4 snatched (15)	**d** moving the hand from side to side
5 unaware (22)	**e** becomes attached
6 waving (62)	**f** not conscious or knowing

3 In sentences **1–8** below complete each of the spaces with the appropriate form of one of the words in **2**.

1 As she walked out of the hotel, a man _____ her bag from her and ran off.
2 We used to use an old washing-up liquid bottle to _____ water at each other.
3 She was shouting excitedly, _____ her certificate in the air.
4 _____ that he was being filmed by a CCTV camera, McGuire broke into the shop.
5 She sat on some chewing gum and it _____ to her jeans.
6 He _____ at the door and told me to get out of his office.

4 In the reading text find two expressions, collocations or phrasal verbs for each of the following verbs. Don't forget to include any dependent prepositions or other words which are used. Two examples have been done for you.

get	*in touch with someone*	_____
hold	*one's nose*	_____
pick	_____	_____
take	_____	_____
make	_____	_____
have	_____	_____

5 Complete each of the spaces below with **two** words from the text.

1 Can you get _____ with Alex and ask him if he's coming on Friday?
2 Keep close to me and hold _____ your bag; there are a lot of pickpockets.
3 I dropped all my books in the street and a kind man helped me pick _____ .
4 John took _____ a Greek restaurant last night. We had a wonderful meal.
5 I made _____ of lending some money to Alan. He still hasn't paid me back.
6 'Do you know where Simon is?' 'No, I'm sorry. I have _____ .'

tyre. Naturally I pulled over to investigate the puncture and in the few seconds I was out of the car my handbag was stolen. By the time I realized this, they had driven off in their car and I was completely helpless. The police informed me that it was a common technique.'

And **William Walker** reports an incident that occurred on a visit to Madrid: 'I made the mistake one morning of looking at a tourist map just near the entrance to the Plaza Mayor. A few minutes later a young man walked towards me and dropped some coins at my feet. As I helped him pick them up, a pickpocket took my wallet which was inside my buttoned-up back pocket. All this happened in the space of seconds and I didn't feel a thing. Not until I got back to my hotel in the evening did I realize what had happened. Luckily I had left my credit cards in the hotel so I didn't suffer too much inconvenience, but I was left feeling angry and paranoid for what remained of my stay.'

50 **Steven Nicholls** tells of an incident in Italy: 'I was in Florence and preparing to move to Venice. I had been to the station to check the train times for the next day and was walking back towards my hotel when two women approached and pushed a newspaper under my eyes.
55 They spoke quickly and excitedly, pointing violently at a photograph in the paper; I had no idea what they were on about so I just smiled and moved on. A sixth sense made me feel for my wallet, which, of course, was gone.

60 'Naturally, the women had disappeared, but a man was hurrying towards me waving my wallet! He turned out to be a local who had seen what was happening and had managed to snatch the wallet back from them. All it cost
65 me was a Campari and soda.'

Vocabulary

Wordlist on page 204 of the Coursebook

A Crime

Match each of the following descriptions with a crime from the box.

burglary	blackmail	pickpocketing	kidnap
smuggling	arson	robbery	drug trafficking

1 By the time he realized his wallet was missing, it was too late. The bus had stopped and the two men had run off in different directions. _____
2 Police have found evidence which suggests the building may have been burned down by an ex-employee who was sacked from the company three months ago. _____
3 Three armed men, each wearing a stocking over his head, ordered the customers to lie still on the floor while the cashier emptied the safe. _____
4 We must have left a window open. They took the DVD player, the television and all my jewellery. The neighbours didn't hear a thing. _____
5 Mrs Brandon received a note demanding £1 million in return for the release of her husband. _____
6 To escape detection he would go to the local cyber café to email his demands. He wanted regular monthly payments of £3,000 in return for his silence over the politician's affair with his secretary. _____
7 For two years he had been illegally taking religious icons and other art treasures out of the country in order to sell them to art collectors in Western Europe. _____
8 Police suspected that most of his fortune came from trading in narcotics, yet they had difficulty proving it. _____

B Phrasal verbs

Phrasal verb list on pages 122 and 123

1 Use the following verbs and particles to make phrasal verbs which have the same meanings as the definitions in **1–8**.

Verbs:	take	make	look	get		
Particles:	up	in	out	up to	into	away with

1 trick or deceive _____
2 investigate _____
3 not be punished for something _____
4 see, hear or understand with difficulty _____
5 invent (a story, an excuse) _____
6 start doing _____
7 admire and respect _____
8 do things you know you shouldn't _____

2 Complete the gaps with the appropriate forms of the phrasal verbs above.

1 Is this story true or are you _____ it _____ ?
2 I couldn't _____ what he was saying. I think he was drunk.
3 He said he'd been robbed and needed some money for a taxi, but I wasn't _____ by his story.
4 You're a fool if you think you can drive so fast all the time and _____ it.
5 The police are _____ the causes of the accident.
6 Are you in trouble with the police again? What have you been _____ this time?

Language focus

Grammar reference on pages 213 and 214 of the Coursebook

A Active and passive

Complete each of the gaps with an appropriate active or passive form of the verb in brackets. You may need to use more than one word in each gap.

1 Glenn Lambert _____ (release) from prison yesterday, ten years after _____ (find) guilty of a crime he _____ (not commit).

2 Our car _____ (repair) at the garage at the moment. I _____ (tell) yesterday that it probably _____ (not be) ready until next Friday.

3 **a:** I _____ (ask) to give a talk at the conference next month.
 b: So have I. I _____ (not prepare) mine yet. How about you?

4 **a:** What _____ (happen) to those boys who _____ (catch) spraying paint on the walls of the school last year?
 b: Don't you remember? They _____ (make) to clean it all off. It _____ (take) them three days altogether.

5 Three million chocolate bars _____ (produce) at this factory each week. Over one million of these _____ (sell) in the UK, and the rest _____ _____ (export) to other European countries.

6 My great grandfather _____ (give) a beautiful clock when he retired in 1960. When he _____ (die) in 1980, the clock _____ (stop) working; it still _____ (not fix).

7 A Roman necklace, which _____ (think) to be worth over two million pounds, _____ (find) last week by Audrey Perham while she _____ (walk) her dog in Queen's Park, Brighton.

8 There were two of them, both about ten years old. They came into my garden and _____ (destroy) all the flowers. The police _____ (not do) anything. It's not right – they shouldn't _____ (allow) to get away with it!

B Revision: Modal verbs

Complete each of the spaces with one of the negative modal forms from the box, together with the correct form of the verb in brackets. More than one answer may be possible.

| mustn't | don't need to | shouldn't | needn't |
| don't have to | didn't need to | didn't have to | needn't have |

1 What a waste of time! I _____ (revise) 16th century European history; none of it came up in the exam.
2 We _____ (pay) for a babysitter for Luke last night; my parents looked after him at their house.
3 The Christmas holidays are a little longer than usual this year. We _____ (go) back to school until January 10th.
4 You _____ (tell) anyone what I've just said. I'll be very angry if you do.
5 I know I _____ (have) any more cream cakes, but it is my birthday after all.
6 I realize now, of course, that I _____ (buy) all this wine for the party; we've got a lot of bottles left from the last one we had.
7 You _____ (worry) about your car while you're away on holiday. We'll look after it for you.
8 He _____ (go) to prison in the end. The judge let him off with a £900 fine.

Use of English

Transformations

Complete the second sentence so that it has a similar meaning to the first sentence, using the word given. **Do not change the word given.** You must use between **two** and **five** words, including the word given. There is an example at the beginning **(0)**.

0 My friends have invited me to their wedding.
   INVITED
   I _____*have been invited*_____ to my friends' wedding.

1 No one gave me any help with the homework.
   NOT
   I _____ any help with the homework.

2 Someone is meeting him at the station.
   MET
   He _____ at the station.

3 Thieves stole all her priceless jewels.
   ROBBED
   She _____ all her priceless jewels.

4 The police are investigating her disappearance.
   LOOKED
   Her disappearance _____ by the police.

5 The witness had invented the whole story.
   MADE
   The whole story _____ the witness.

6 People say swimming is good exercise for your back.
   SAID
   Swimming _____ good exercise for your back.

7 People expect that tax cuts will be announced today.
   BE
   Tax cuts _____ today.

8 People believe he won a lot of money on the lottery.
   BELIEVED
   He _____ won a lot of money on the lottery.

9 They think the burglar knew the owner of the house.
   KNOWN
   The burglar _____ the owner of the house.

10 I took my coat but it wasn't necessary as it didn't rain.
   HAVE
   I _____ my coat as it didn't rain.

11 Fortunately, it wasn't necessary for us to go shopping last weekend.
   NEED
   Fortunately, _____ go shopping last weekend.

What to expect in the exam

Remember in the exam you have to write your answers on a separate sheet. You should write only the missing words, not the whole sentence.

FCE Part 3

Word formation

Use the word given in capitals at the end of each line to form a word that fits in the gap **in the same line**. There is an example at the beginning (0).

CCTV cameras

Close circuit television cameras are **(0)** _increasingly_ becoming	**INCREASE**
a fact of life in modern Britain. They can be seen in office	
(1) _____ , shopping centres, banks,	**BUILD**
(2) _____ areas and even parks, and it is estimated	**RESIDENT**
that the average Briton is filmed an **(3)** _____ 200 times	**AMAZE**
a day. It is believed that CCTV leads to a **(4)** _____ in	**REDUCE**
certain types of crime, such as car theft, **(5)** _____ and	**ROB**
street violence. Its supporters defend it as an **(6)** _____	**EFFECT**
way of improving security in town centres, and of helping to	
bring **(7)** _____ to justice. Civil liberties groups, who	**CRIME**
object to the **(8)** _____ of CCTV cameras, feel that they	**PRESENT**
constitute a serious **(9)** _____ of privacy and say that	**INVADE**
there is little **(10)** _____ that they reduce offending.	**EVIDENT**

FCE Part 2

Open cloze

Read the text below and think of the word which best fits each gap. Use only **one** word in each gap. There is an example at the beginning (0).

House-sitters

Nowadays **(0)** ___there___ are far too many stories of homeowners **(1)** _____

have been away on holiday and come home to find that their house

(2) _____ been broken into. Unfortunately, simply locking the doors and

cancelling the newspapers is **(3)** _____ enough to keep out burglars.

A much better way to prevent your home from **(4)** _____ burgled is to

employ a professional house-sitter, either through an agency **(5)** _____ as

'Homesitters', **(6)** _____ by placing an advertisement in a magazine like *The

Lady*. House-sitters are paid around £10 a day, including a food allowance, to live in

a house while **(7)** _____ owners are away. An extra charge **(8)** _____

made if the house-sitter is required to **(9)** _____ care of one or more pets.

Agencies, which charge a considerable fee for their services, accept full responsibility

(10) _____ anything which might go wrong. House-sitters

(11) _____ therefore chosen very carefully; as well as the usual interview

and personal references, inquiries are **(12)** _____ about any previous criminal

convictions.

Writing

Informal letters

Read the following Writing Part 2 instructions and the two answers which were written by students. Which letter do you think would be given a higher mark?

You have just returned from a holiday abroad, during which something of yours was stolen. Write a letter to your penfriend, telling him/her about the incident and what you did to try to recover the stolen item.

Write your **letter** in **120–180** words.

Student A

Dear Paul

I arrive to the station to caught the train to the airport. I feeling sad because of I finish my holiday. I enjoyed with the holiday very much and I didn't want to come to home.

I have decided to go to the shop for to buy some sweets and make me felt happier. I put my suitcase to the ground and paid to the woman for the sweets. I wanted to pick up my suitcase but it was not there any more! Where was my suitcase? What a shock! Somebody stealed it.

Consequently, I feeling sadder. It was a horrible way to finish of a holiday.

Helmut Braun

Student B

Dear Esther

How are you? Did you get my postcard from Italy? You'll never guess what happened to me after I'd posted it to you!

I was walking down the main street on my way to the beach when I heard everyone shouting behind me. I looked round and there on the pavement coming towards me was a young man on a motor scooter. Before I knew what was happening, he had snatched my bag and was riding off into the distance.

I started to run after him but it was useless – you know how unfit I am! Anyway, at that moment a car pulled over beside me and the driver, who had seen the incident, told me to get in. We chased after the thief, and as soon as he realized he was being followed, he dropped the bag and disappeared.

You can imagine how relieved I felt. And I was so grateful to the driver – thanks to him my holiday wasn't ruined.

How about you, Esther? Did anything exciting happen on your holiday? Write and tell me all about it.

Lots of love

Angela

A Analysis

Now read the two letters again and then answer Yes or No to the following questions about each one.

	A	B
Content		
1 Has the writer answered all parts of the question?		
Organization and cohesion		
2 Is the letter organized into suitable paragraphs?		
3 Are ideas connected with appropriate linking words?		
4 Does the letter have an appropriate beginning and ending?		
Range and accuracy		
5 Is there a good range of vocabulary?		
6 Has the writer used a variety of tenses?		
7 Is the English reasonably accurate?		
Style and format		
8 Is the letter written in an informal style?		
9 Is the answer clearly set out as a letter?		
Target reader		
10 Would the reader understand what happened and know what the writer did to try to recover the stolen item?		

B Accuracy

Look back at Student A's answer. Find the following mistakes and correct them:

a eight mistakes related to verb forms, eg *I arrived*

b eight mistakes related to the incorrect use of prepositions, eg **at** *the station*

C Addressing the reader

Look back at Student B's answer. Underline those sentences in which the writer talks directly to the reader of the letter.

Example:
How are you?

D Writing task

Now write your own answer to the question.

> ### Don't forget!
>
> - Set your answer out as an informal letter.
>   Include suitable opening and closing paragraphs.
>   See page 10 in Unit 1 of the Coursebook for useful language.
> - Use a range of vocabulary and structures when describing what happened.
>   See pages 50 and 51 in Unit 4 of the Coursebook for the ingredients of a good narrative.
> - Organize your ideas into logical paragraphs. You could have one paragraph to describe how the item was stolen and another to say how you tried to recover it.

Reading

FCE Part 2

Gapped text

1 You are going to read a newspaper article about a man who teaches survival techniques. Seven sentences have been removed from the article. Choose from the sentences **A–H** the one which fits each space **(1–7)**. There is one extra sentence which you do not need to use.

The man who can survive anywhere

Ray Mears tells Graham Hadley how learning survival skills can help us rediscover nature.

Armed with little more than a hunting knife and a cooking pot Ray Mears can survive anywhere. He loves nothing more than spending days, weeks or even months alone in the wild, and he will talk passionately about any aspect of the natural world, from his favourite trees to endangered species of animals.

1 ☐ Those who sign up for the courses range from children to grandparents, with a large number of twenty to thirty-year-olds looking for a taste of adventure.

'People might see it as survival skills,' he says, 'but I aim to teach a little more than that. I try to show people how to reconnect with nature, how to see it in a different light. Some who have participated on the course have experienced a very profound change in their life. They develop a greater awareness of nature. They return to the cities and notice the seasons change for the first time. **2 ☐** The city and their life in it are transformed.'

The Woodlore courses take participants to experience tribal life with the native people of Namibia, or to shiver through an Arctic survival course in Lapland. **3 ☐** These are the places to fulfil the schoolboy dream of lighting fires with just a couple of sticks.

4 ☐ 'There are lots of simple survival tips, like it's often better to avoid anything which is green. More energy is used up eating it than you get out of it. Roots are best because you need carbohydrates.'

There is a very serious purpose to what Mears does. 'All around the world cultures are losing ancient skills as the latest generation is attracted away from the land to an easy life through technology,' he explains. 'We live in a world where we can have whatever we want, but along the way we have lost contact with the natural world. **5 ☐** Without them, there's a danger we could lose sight of where we've come from.'

'The area around London is particularly threatened. **6 ☐** People need places where they can get close to nature.'

But Mears is not against the latest technological developments and is well aware of the benefits. **7 ☐** 'In this way people can become part of a global tribe, one which lives both for and from the natural world.' *www.raymears.com*

A Mears even takes groups to visit a highly-protected nature reserve in Canada to watch bear cubs being born and raised.

B He has just hired an internet consultancy firm to design a website which will give people all over the globe access to his knowledge.

C This experience, and others like it, led Mears to write *The Survival Handbook*, which was published in 1989.

D The ancient woodlands should be left alone, and areas not needed for agriculture should be planted with trees and allowed to grow wild.

E They see the geese, the pigeons, the edible plants growing between the cracks in the pavement.

F These ancient skills help to put us back in touch with nature, and to understand our place in the world.

G He also teaches how to identify edible plants for food.

H His passions are reflected in Woodlore, a series of courses in which he passes on survival techniques to people of all ages.

2   Use the word given in capitals at the end of some of the lines to form a word that fits in the gap **in the same line**. All the words you require appeared in the reading text. There is an example at the beginning (**0**).

0 Global warming is thought to be responsible for some of the
world's recent ___*natural*___ disasters.   **NATURE**

1 We took part in a demonstration yesterday to protest against the
construction of two new housing ___developments___ on the edge of town.   **DEVELOP**

2 The creation of nature reserves will help to ensure the
___survival___ of many endangered species.   **SURVIVE**

3 There were over 350 ___participants___ on the Environmental
Skills course.   **PARTICIPATE**

4 He spoke ___passionately___ about the need to protect the tiger's
natural habitat.   **PASSION**

5 Deforestation in South America is an issue of ___global___
importance.   **GLOBE**

6 You can't really go ___anywhere___ in the countryside nowadays
without seeing some evidence of Man's influence.   **WHERE**

7 The council intends to raise ___awareness___ of the effects of
traffic pollution on our health.   **AWARE**

8 Recent ___technological___ advances such as the Internet are proving **TECHNOLOGY**
very useful for conservationists.

3   In numbers **1–3** in excercise **2** you needed to use the suffixes *-ment*, *-al* and *-ant* to form the appropriate nouns. Use these same suffixes to form nouns from the following verbs. The first two have been done for you.

Verb	Noun	Verb	Noun
arrive	*arrival*	enjoy	
consult	*consultant*	replace	
entertain	entertainment	approve	
refuse	refusal	deny	denial
assist	assistance	arrange	
occupy		inhabit	

4   Complete each of the gaps with the correct form of one of the nouns in exercise **3**.

1   All 540 _inhabitants_ of the village of Poynings had to be evacuated because of the forest fire.

2   The Government has given its _approval_ for the construction of a new by-pass for Oldbury. Road works will start next April.

3   The views were fantastic but the constant noise of the motorway did rather ruin our _enjoyment_ of the walk.

4   Conservationists were not convinced by the Minister's _denial_ that radioactive waste had been dumped at sea.

5   Fortunately, none of the _occupants_ of the car was injured in the crash.

Vocabulary

Wordlist on pages 204 and 205 of the Coursebook

A   Crossword: The weather

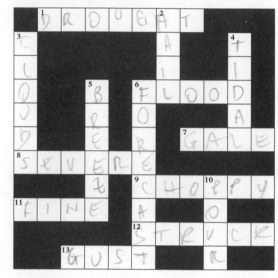

Across

1   a long period of time without rain

6   a large amount of water covering an area which is normally dry

7   a very strong wind

8   a _____ storm is a very bad one

9   a _____ sea has lots of small waves caused by the wind

11   _____ rain consists of very small raindrops

12   'Several trees were _____ by lightning during the storm.'

13   a _____ is a short, sudden period of strong wind

Down

2   small hard balls of frozen rain

3   'Look at those thick, black _____ – I think it's going to rain.'

4   'After the earthquake came a _____ wave, which destroyed several houses on the coast.'

5   a gentle _breeze_ is a very light wind

6   'You can't always rely on the weather _____ to predict the weather accurately.'

10   'to _____ with rain' means 'to rain very heavily'

B   The environment

1   Match each sentence beginning **1–6** with an appropriate ending **a–f**.

1   One of the aims of Greenpeace is to **raise**

2   I strongly believe that anyone caught **dropping**

3   The ship's captain denied he had been **dumping**

4   Several species of birds and animals **face**

5   The local authorities talk of the need to **recycle**

6   Not enough is being done to **preserve**

a   **extinction** in this country as a result of modern farming methods.

b   **paper**, but they have not provided enough containers to enable us to do this.

c   **awareness** of the environmental problems facing our planet.

d   **litter** should be ordered to pay a heavy fine.

e   **wildlife** in this country.

f   **waste** of any kind at sea.

2 Match the words **1–8** with the words **a–h** to form compound nouns.

1 bottle	**a** effect
2 dog	**b** pollution
3 greenhouse	**c** reserve
4 oil	**d** mess
5 traffic	**e** bank
6 exhaust	**f** slick
7 power	**g** station
8 nature	**h** fumes

3 Complete each of the gaps with one of the compound nouns from exercise **2**.

1 _____ are responsible for a great deal of the pollution in our cities.

2 The huge _____ is moving slowly towards Ireland, and several miles of coastline are under threat.

3 It's almost impossible to walk on the pavement in this city without stepping in _____ .

4 Global warming is caused by the _____ , the result of an increase in the amount of carbon dioxide and other gases in the Earth's atmosphere.

5 Environmentalists have been protesting at the construction of a new nuclear _____ _____ on the outskirts of the city.

6 Wildlife enthusiasts have called for the area to be made a _____ in order to protect the rare species of butterfly which lives there.

Language focus

Grammar reference on pages 214 and 215 of the Coursebook

A *So*, *neither* and *nor*

1 Match each statement **1–8** with a reply **a–h**.

1 She doesn't like that type of music.	**a** So would I.
2 We didn't enjoy the film.	**b** I'm not.
3 I went swimming last night.	**c** Neither does he.
4 My favourite food is pasta.	**d** So did my brother.
5 She's never been abroad.	**e** Neither did they.
6 I'd rather go to the cinema.	**f** We don't.
7 He's going to the demonstration.	**g** Neither have I.
8 I have to do a lot of homework tonight.	**h** So is mine.

2 Complete each of the gaps below with *so* or *neither/nor* and an appropriate auxiliary verb. The first one has been done for you.

1 He can't drive and __*neither can*__ I.

2 I'm older than Harry, and _So is_ Ron.

3 He never writes to me, and _neither does_ Colin.

4 Her parents are going to France, and _so are_ mine.

5 Seamus came to the party, and _so did_ Dean.

6 Hermione won't tell anyone, and _neither will_ I.

7 I've already seen that film, and _so has_ Neville.

8 I wouldn't be happy if you went alone, and _neither would_ your father.

9 I'd better go to bed, and _so had_ you, young man.

B Conditionals

1 Complete the gaps in the following sentences with the appropriate form of the verb in brackets. The first one has been done for you.

  1 If I _had_ (have) more time, I _would help_ (help) you, but I'm afraid I'm just too busy.

  2 I _____ (buy) you a new pair of football boots as long as you _____ (promise) to look after them properly.

  3 Why did you tell your parents? If you _____ (not/say) anything, we _____ (not/get) into trouble.

  4 If he _____ (sleep) for less than eight hours, he _____ (usually/be) bad-tempered all morning.

  5 It's a shame you weren't at the party. If you _____ (go), you _____ (meet) my sister.

  6 If we _____ (beat) United next Saturday, we _____ (go) to the top of the league.

  7 There's a quicker way to do it. If you _____ (press) 'control' and 'U', it _____ (underline) your work as you type.

  8 If I _____ (be) you, I _____ (go) to the doctor's.

  9 We _____ (be) there by 6 o'clock this evening unless we _____ (get) stuck in a traffic jam.

  10 I had to wait two hours to see the doctor. If I _____ (not/take) my book with me to read, I _____ (get) so bored.

2 Rewrite sentences below to form second, third or mixed conditional sentences. The first one has been done for you.

  1 I don't have to pay to get into the museum because I'm unemployed.

    If I wasn't unemployed, I'd have to pay to get into the museum.

  2 We didn't go sailing because there wasn't enough wind.

  3 We don't go abroad on holiday because I'm afraid of flying.

  4 He's broken his leg so he can't drive.

  5 I couldn't take any photos because I forgot to pack my camera.

  6 He isn't going to the wedding because he hasn't got a suit.

  7 He's feeling ill because he drank too much last night.

  8 She didn't pass her exams so she couldn't go to university.

  9 They didn't watch the news so they didn't hear about the earthquake.

3 Complete each of the following sentences in an appropriate way.

  1 If I had to spend a year living abroad, I _____ .

  2 If I had the power to change one thing in my country, I _____ .

  3 I probably wouldn't have met my best friend if _____ .

  4 I'd be really pleased if _____ .

  5 If someone gives me some money for my birthday, _____ .

  6 If the computer hadn't been invented, _____ .

Use of English

FCE Part 1

Multiple-choice cloze

For questions **1–12**, read the text below and decide which answer (**A**, **B**, **C** or **D**) best fits each space. There is an example at the beginning (**0**).

Global warming

Few people now (**0**) _question_ the reality of global warming and its effects on the world's climate. Many scientists (**1**) _____ the blame for recent natural disasters on the increase in the world's temperatures and are convinced that, more than (**2**) _____ before, the earth is at (**3**) _____ from the forces of the wind, rain and sun. (**4**) _____ to them, global warming is making extreme weather events, such as hurricanes and droughts, even more (**5**) _____ and causing sea levels all around the world to (**6**) _____ .

Environmental groups are putting (**7**) _____ on governments to take action to reduce the amount of carbon dioxide which is given (**8**) _____ by factories and power plants, thus attacking the problem at its source. They are in (**9**) _____ of more money being spent on research into solar, wind and wave energy devices, which could then replace existing power (**10**) _____ .

Some scientists, (**11**) _____ , believe that even if we stopped releasing carbon dioxide and other gases into the atmosphere tomorrow, we would have to wait (**12**) _____ hundred years to notice the results. Global warming, it seems, is here to stay.

	A	B	C	D
0	hesitate	question	disagree	concern
1	give	put	take	have
2	yet	never	once	ever
3	threat	danger	risk	harm
4	Concerning	Regarding	Depending	According
5	strict	severe	strong	heavy
6	raise	arise	rise	lift
7	force	pressure	persuasion	encouragement
8	off	away	up	over
9	belief	request	favour	suggestion
10	factories	generations	houses	stations
11	but	although	despite	however
12	several	over	numerous	various

FCE Part 4

Transformations

Complete the second sentence so that it has a similar meaning to the first sentence, using the word given. **Do not change the word given.** You must use between **two** and **five** words, including the word given.

1 Both Christina and Fiona enjoyed the film.
   SO
   Christina enjoyed the film and ___so did___ Fiona.

2 I'm going to stay at John's for the night.
   PUT
   John's going to ___PUT ME UP___ for the night.

3 They had to postpone the concert until September.
   PUT
   They had to _____ until September.

4 You need to spend longer on your homework.
   TIME
   You need to put ___more time into___ your homework.

5 We've had some heavy rain recently.
   RAINING
   It ___has been raining___ recently.

6 We'll only go swimming if the weather improves.
   UNLESS
   We ___won't go swimming___ the weather improves.

7 I can't afford to go to the cinema.
   ENOUGH
   If I _____ , I'd go to the cinema.

8 I only knew he'd got married because his brother told me.
   NOT
   I wouldn't have known he'd got married if ___his brother___ me.

Writing

FCE Part 2

Articles

1 Read the following Writing Part 2 question and the model below.

You see this announcement in an international magazine:

Write your **article** for the magazine.

WRITING COMPETITION

The Best and the Worst

The theme of our writing competition this month is **The Weather**.

Write an article about your favourite and least favourite weather conditions, telling our readers why you feel the way you do.

The best article will be published in the magazine and the writer will receive £250.

The highs and lows of mountain weather

If you lived in the mountains like me, what would be your favourite type of weather? Glorious sunshine to sunbathe in? Deep snow to ski in?

Surprisingly, perhaps, it's the rain I most enjoy. Whether it's fine or heavy, spitting or pouring, I love wet weather! The rain on my face as I walk across the fields is cool and refreshing and always puts me in a good mood. It makes me feel optimistic about the future: after the rain, the sun comes out; after a shower the countryside is greener; and after my walk there's the promise of a warm fire and a cup of hot cocoa.

And what would you find it hard to put up with? Where I live it's the wind, which blows almost continuously for two weeks every August. Clothes are blown off washing lines, tiles are pulled off roofs and activities such as walking and cycling become very difficult. Who wouldn't feel bad-tempered by the end of it all?

But whatever the weather, I know I'd hate it if it was always the same.

2 The model is written in a more informal style. Find examples in the article of the following features.

Features	Examples
• A relevant title	*The highs and lows of mountain weather*
• Questions to involve the reader	_____
• A range of vocabulary related to the weather	_____
	_____
• Elements of informal language eg *contractions, phrasal verbs, linking words*	_____
	_____
• Examples to illustrate a point	_____
• Adverbs expressing opinion or attitude	_____

3 Either: **a** Write your own answer to the question in 1 on page 88
   or   **b** Write an answer to **one** of the following questions.

1 You see this announcement in an international magazine:

> **COMPETITION**
>
> Write an article about a situation when you experienced severe weather conditions, telling our readers how you were affected by them.
>
> The best article will win a prize of £500.

Write your **article** for the competition.

2 You see this notice in an international magazine:

> **PEOPLE AND PLACES**
> We are looking for articles on the following question:
> *How does the climate in your country affect the way people feel and behave?*
> The best article will be published in our magazine.

Write your **article** for the magazine.

Before you write

● Read more about writing articles on pages 129 and 130 of the Coursebook.
● Read the following advice about style and do the exercise below.
Formal and Informal Style: consistency
In each of the questions above, the article will be written for readers of an international magazine. The style of your writing can be either more formal or more informal, but it must be consistent throughout the article; in other words, you should not mix formal and informal language in the same piece of writing.

4 The following extracts **a–c** were each written in answer to one of the three writing questions above. Match each extract to one of the questions. Which of the extracts is **not** written in a consistent style?

a
> I've never really been keen on going out in the snow – and I can't understand why people get so excited about it. Your feet get soaking wet, your fingers nearly freeze off, and where's the fun in having a snowball pushed down the back of your neck? I'd love to have enough money to be able to get away from here when it snows.

b
> Moreover, the combination of harsh winters and warm summers has an interesting effect on the personality of those who live in the more remote, rural parts of my country. Inhabitants of these areas tend to withdraw into themselves between December and March, becoming shy and reserved. In spring, however, they undergo a transformation – it's really amazing! They're just so incredibly different – you'd almost think you were in another country!

c
> Huge waves crashed onto the beach, sending sand and stones high into the air. Gale-force winds caused destruction to buildings along the seafront, and made walking in the street extremely hazardous. We spent the day sheltering in the lounge area of our hotel, wondering when, if ever, the storm would die down.

Reading

FCE Part 1

Multiple choice

1 You are going to read a magazine article about a chef. For questions **1–8**, choose the answer (**A**, **B**, **C** or **D**) which you think fits best according to the text.

Meals on *wheels*

Sheila Keating meets the Ferrari team chef at a Formula One race.

It's Grand Prix weekend, and as the stars of Formula One race against the clock to give themselves the best starting position for the big event
5 tomorrow, a different race against time is under way. In miniature makeshift kitchens alongside the track, the team chefs are busy preparing lunch for the mechanics
10 and drivers.

Claudio Degli Esposti is in charge of the cooking for all 60 Ferrari team members, plus their personal weekend guests, who could bring the
15 numbers up to 80. 'It's a huge honour to be chef of the Ferrari team,' he says. 'I get on really well with the guys, and they make me feel part of things. Also you have the chance to
20 travel all over the world. I don't see a great deal of the racing,' he says, laughing, 'but the TV monitor is on just outside the kitchen, so I know what's going on.'

25 The food he prepares for the team is typical of his region in Italy, Emilia Romagna, where the team is based: lasagne, tortelloni, tortellini, ravioli. 'There are usually two different
30 pastas, two or three kinds of meat, plenty of side dishes,' he explains. It is left to others to say that the food

at Ferrari is the envy of other teams. Degli Esposti simply shrugs his
35 shoulders and smiles. 'Italians enjoy eating good food. It is a way of life, so even if your focus is on winning the world championship, you must still have good food.'

40 The drivers, of course, have their own long-term food agenda, tailored to the stresses of competition. With temperatures in the cockpit of a Formula One car sometimes 15
45 degrees hotter than that outside, it is not unusual for a driver to lose three kilos in fluid during a race, unless he has the right balance of fluid and carbohydrate. Driver Michael
50 Schumacher, with his reputation for formidable fitness, is attended at all times by Balbir Singh, who looks after his diet and exercise. 'Before qualifying and racing, Michael eats
55 the food prepared by Singh,' says Degli Esposti, 'usually something very light, but afterwards he eats the same food as the rest of the team.'

Unlike many of the team kitchens,
60 which contain stacks of tins and jars, Degli Esposti's has a large fridge filled with different types of cheese, ham, sausages, vegetables and fruit. The emphasis is on simple food
65 prepared carefully. 'In the beginning it was very difficult, working in a very

small kitchen, without a lot of the things a chef is used to. And finding ingredients was a problem. Now I
70 know the places to shop at near every track, and I know I can get anything I need. I love to cook fish and meat, but unless I can get the best, I don't touch it.'

75 Lunch is spread out as a buffet. On a table at one end of the eating area there are salads of mozzarella and tomatoes, carpaccio topped with truffles, Italian sausages and
80 courgettes, a chicken dish with rosemary potatoes, and tortellini tossed in a sauce of cheese and cream. 'I always try to get as much as possible prepared early, so I have only
85 the hot dishes to do at the last minute,' explains Degli Esposti. The mechanics come in first, followed closely by the drivers. Eddie Irvine heads straight for the truffles, while
90 Schumacher wanders into the kitchen to see what's cooking.

Lunch over, everyone disperses, full of praise for the chef. Degli Esposti gives a small wave of appreciation and
95 immediately starts clearing away. 'I have many friends in Italy,' he says quietly, 'who think I have the best job in the world.'

1 The kitchens at the Formula One meeting in the article
  A are not completely ready yet.
  B are overcrowded.
  C are close to the racing action.
  D are not fully equipped.

2 What does Degli Esposti enjoy about his job?
  A He can see motor racing all over the world.
  B He likes being a member of a team.
  C He can travel around the countries he visits.
  D He is a fan of Formula One racing.

3 What does the writer mean when she says that the drivers 'have their own long-term food agenda' in lines 40 and 41?
  A They spend a lot of time eating.
  B They eat the same things all season.
  C They go for long periods without eating.
  D They follow a carefully planned diet.

4 Schumacher eats food prepared by Balbir Singh because
  A he prefers it to Degli Esposti's.
  B it forms an important part of his preparation for a race.
  C it has an excellent reputation.
  D it contains more fluids and carbohydrates than Degli Esposti's.

5 The food in Degli Esposti's kitchen, compared to that in other teams' kitchens, is
  A fresher.
  B easier to cook.
  C more varied.
  D less fattening.

6 What does Degli Esposti insist on when he is cooking for the Ferrari team?
  A nearby shops
  B a big kitchen
  C the highest quality food
  D a large fridge

7 When the members of the Ferrari team have lunch
  A they go into the kitchen to get their food.
  B they all eat at the same table.
  C they serve themselves.
  D they each eat a number of different dishes.

8 Which adjective would the writer use to describe Degli Esposti?
  A modest
  B shy
  C arrogant
  D moody

2 Complete the gaps with an appropriate preposition. The words in **bold** appear in the text.

1 It was a **race** ___against___ **time** to get the menus printed in time for the opening.
2 In a restaurant the maitre d' is the person ___in___ **charge** ___of___ all the waiters.
3 It's **typical** ___for___ you to order the most expensive dish in the restaurant!
4 Welcome to *Food Matters*. In tonight's programme the **focus** is ___on___ Mediterranean food.
5 John has a **reputation** ___for___ eating too quickly.
6 Ravioli is usually **filled** ___with___ minced meat or cheese.
7 The **emphasis** in this restaurant is ___on___ quality, not quantity.
8 All the wedding guests were full of **praise** ___for___ the chef.

Vocabulary

Wordlist on page 205 of the Coursebook

A   Food

Which word could be used to describe the food in each of the following cases? Match each of the words in the box to a statement. The first one has been done for you.

spicy	rich	bitter	sour	stodgy	sickly	crunchy	bland	savoury	greasy

1 This coffee really needs a little more sugar adding to it.   ___bitter___
2 There's rather a lot of fat on these chips.   _____
3 How many litres of cream did you put in this sauce?   _____
4 No, it's not a sweet dish. It's got salt and a few herbs in it.   _____
5 I'm sorry, I don't like this – it's like eating a lemon.   _____
6 That chocolate mousse was far too sweet – it made me feel quite ill.   _____
7 Sorry about the noise – this celery's just so fresh.   _____
8 I'm not very keen on curry; it's too hot for me.   _____
9 The food in our school canteen is very heavy; it takes ages to digest.   _____
10 It hasn't really got a lot of flavour, has it?   _____

B Health

Read the definitions below, then complete each gap **1–6** with an appropriate form of one of the words.

wound (n)
a cut or hole in the body, often caused by a gun, knife or other weapon. (verb: wound)

injury (n)
harm caused to a person, often as the result of an accident (verb: injure)

damage (n)
harm caused to things (verb: damage)

ache (n)
a dull continuous pain (verb: ache)

pain (n)
usually more extreme discomfort than ache, caused by injury or illness

hurt (v)
to cause pain to (part of) a person

1 A total of sixteen houses were _____ in the explosion.
2 Let go of my arm – you're _____ me!
3 Take an aspirin if your head _____ .
4 The robbers shot at security guards, killing one and seriously _____ another.
5 Several people received serious _____ in the train crash.
6 He complained of chest _____ and breathing difficulties – a sure sign of pneumonia.

C *Have, put, give* and *take*

Match each sentence beginning on the left with a suitable ending on the right.

1 He had both	**a** plaster on her cut.
2 He had another	**b** an injection in his leg.
3 They put him	**c** own temperature.
4 She put a	**d** operation on his leg.
5 They gave him	**e** his legs in plaster for six weeks.
6 He gave her	**f** pill for her headache.
7 She took a	**g** on a course of antibiotics.
8 He took his	**h** a prescription, which she took to the chemist's.

D Word formation: Nouns

In one word in each of the groups of four below, the wrong suffix has been used to form the noun. Find the word and write the correct form.

Example:

		frequency	
0 ignorance	significance	*frequance*	resistance

1 tiredness	involveness	friendliness	uselessness
2 inconvenience	impatience	disappearence	disobedience
3 announcement	replacement	measurement	obligement
4 seriosity	generosity	curiosity	anxiety
5 explanation	complication	comparation	investigation
6 soreness	popularness	consciousness	healthiness
7 commitment	permitment	excitement	investment
8 security	severity	sincerity	retirity

Language focus

 Grammar reference on pages 215 and 216 of the Coursebook

A Countable and uncountable nouns

Underline the alternative which cannot be used.

1 Have you heard *any/a/the* news about the accident?

2 I didn't speak *a large number/a great deal/a lot* of English when I was in London.

3 *Many/Several/Every* people in our neighbourhood have complained about the smell from the factory.

4 They didn't give us very much *advice/suggestion/information* about where to look for a cheap *guest house/hotel/accommodation* in the town.

5 Could you pass me a *piece/bar/slice* of bread please?

6 **a:** Would you like *some/any/few* more chips?

   b: No, thanks. I've already got *plenty/much/enough*.

7 We haven't got *no/any/much* cheese left. Could you buy *a few/a little/some* on your way home tonight?

8 Come on, let's go out for a meal. We've still got *a little/little/plenty of* money.

9 I think I'll have *some more/another/any more* coffee.

10 Don't put *too much/another/any more* chicken in my sandwiches. A couple of slices is plenty.

B Reported speech

1 Read this extract from a letter which Roger wrote to his penfriend, telling him about an interview for a job he went to recently. Then complete the dialogue below.

> It was a really short interview, but I think I did OK. She started off by asking why I had applied for the job. I explained to her that I was thinking of going to catering college next year and that I wanted to have some experience of hotel or restaurant work first. Then when she asked me if I had any previous experience I told her about a summer holiday I'd spent working behind the bar at the Sussex Hotel. I mentioned something about how useful it had been and how it had helped me to understand what working in a large hotel was like. She seemed quite impressed with that! Anyway, she wanted to know what I thought my main strengths were, so I said I had a lot of patience and that I was very reliable – you know how I always work hard and never arrive late.

Interviewer: So, tell me Roger, **(1)** _____ ?

Roger: Well, **(2)** _____ to catering college next year, and **(3)** _____ some experience of working in a restaurant or hotel before I go.

Interviewer: And **(4)** _____ any previous experience of this type of work?

Roger: Yes, I spent one summer working behind the bar in the restaurant at the Sussex Hotel. It **(5)** _____ . I think it **(6)** _____ to work in a large hotel – the demands of the job, the pressures, the challenges and so on.

Interviewer: Good. Now, let's talk about your personal qualities. **(7)** _____ ?

Roger: Well, I **(8)** _____ , which I think is an important quality for a waiter. And I also think **(9)** _____ person – I always work hard, and I never arrive late for anything.

2 The following comments from two teachers were recorded by Lynda Johnson when doing a survey at school on healthy living. Read the questions and comments and then complete the extract from the report which Lynda wrote a week later.

What do you do to keep fit?

Mr Bracewell: I enjoy all kinds of sport, particularly running – I'm competing in a marathon tomorrow.

Ms Hallam: I do aerobics every morning, but I'm thinking of taking up jogging instead.

Can you give us any advice about what to eat?

Mr Bracewell: Personally, I eat a lot of carbohydrates because of my running, but in general, a balanced diet is the best way to stay healthy.

Ms Hallam: The advice I always give to my students is that they shouldn't eat snacks between meals. And of course, everyone should eat a balanced diet.

Do you think diets are a good way to lose weight?

Mr Bracewell: I don't know – I've never needed to go on one!

Ms Hallam: I went on a diet once and I lost about five kilos. I wouldn't do it again, though – I like eating too much.

Healthy living

As part of a project on healthy living I spoke last week to Mr Bracewell, the French teacher, and Ms Hallam, who teaches biology, and I asked them to comment on various aspects related to this topic.

Firstly, I asked both teachers what **(1)** _____ .
Mr Bracewell said he enjoyed all kinds of sports, particularly running: he added that
(2) _____ . Ms Hallam said
(3) _____ every morning, but that
(4) _____ instead.

When I asked them **(5)** _____ any advice about what to eat, both teachers recommended **(6)** _____ a balanced diet. Ms Hallam said that she always advised **(7)** _____ snacks between meals, and Mr Bracewell commented that he ate a lot of carbohydrates because of his running.

I then asked the teachers **(8)** _____ a good way to lose weight. Mr Bracewell replied that he did not know, because **(9)** _____ . Ms Hallam said that **(10)** _____ and had lost five kilos. She went on to say that **(11)** _____ , however, as she **(12)** _____ too much.

Use of English

FCE Part 2

Open cloze

Read the text below and think of the word which best fits each gap. Use only **one** word in each gap. There is an example at the beginning (0).

Perfect fish and chips

There **(0)** _are_ plenty of fish and chip shops in Hampshire, but **(1)** _few_, if any, are as popular as the one in Eastleigh, not far from Southampton. **(2)** _from_ the time it opens at 5 o'clock until closing time at 9, there is an almost constant queue.

According to the owners, Les and Shirley Armstrong, there are four areas that must be perfect in **(3)** _order_ to achieve great fish and chips. First, of **(4)** _all_ , you need the fish. The Armstrongs **(5)** _do_ not use fresh cod, which Les says goes soft and mushy. Instead, they buy frozen Icelandic cod, **(6)** _which_ is filleted and frozen within three hours of **(7)** _being_ caught. When you fry it, **(8)** _then it_ stays firm and comes apart in lovely white flakes. Next on the list are the potatoes. If you want to make perfect chips, Les suggests you buy potatoes with a low sugar content; too **(9)** _much_ sugar and you end up with greasy, brown chips. Then there is the batter, a mixture of flour, eggs and milk which is used **(10)** _to_ cover the fish before frying it. The Armstrongs dip their fish in a combination of two types of batter; **(11)** _one_ contains hard flour, the other soft. Finally, you need a good beef fat, or 'dripping'; Les and Shirley fry their fish and chips separately in a high-quality deodorised dripping that cannot **(12)** _be_ smelt in the shop.

FCE Part 4

Transformations

Complete the second sentence so that it has a similar meaning to the first sentence, using the word given. **Do not change the word given.** You must use between **two** and **five** words, including the word given.

1 'You must wear a tie,' the teacher told him.
   TO
   The teacher told him he ___has to wear___ a tie.

2 'We were trying to phone you,' they said.
   BEEN
   They said ___they had been trying___ to phone me.

3 'Where did you buy your shoes, Sally?' asked Gail.
   HAD
   Gail asked Sally ___where she had bought her___ shoes.

4 'Don't swim too far out,' she warned him.
   WARNED
   She ___warned him to not___ swim too far out.

5 Sean said I ought to lie down for a while.
   LIE
   Sean suggested ___me lie down___ for a while.

6 She gave me very little help with the homework.
   NOT
   She did ___not help give me___ help with my homework.

Writing

Essays, short stories and informal letters

A Planning

Match the writing questions **1–3** to the paragraph plans **A–C**.

1 You have been doing a class project on food. Your teacher has asked you to write an essay giving your opinions on the following statement:

Parents should let their children eat what they want.

Write your **essay**.

2 You have decided to enter a short-story competition.
The competition rules say that the story must end with the following words:

I will never forget that meal as long as I live.

Write your **story** for the competition.

3 Last weekend several of your relatives came to your home for a family meal to celebrate an important event. Write a letter to your pen friend, telling him/her what you were celebrating and describing the meal. Describe what you ate **and** mention some things that happened during the celebrations. Do not write any addresses.

Write your **letter**.

A

- *'Anniversary meal' – going out together for one year*
- *I arrived late – she was angry*
- *Food took long time to arrive; cold and undercooked*
- *Waiter spilt drinks over us*
- *We argued about something – split up*
- *Finish with words from question*

B

Introduction: importance of food for health. Disagree with **statement**.

a Parents know what is good for children's health; responsibility to guide them. Need to ensure they have balanced diet (give examples).

b Many children would avoid food with vitamins, minerals, proteins.
Fast food, chips, sweets, chocolate: all bad for health, eg sweets cause tooth decay.

c Some children might eat all day – become overweight.
Others might not eat at all – become too thin.

Conclusion: Restate opinion: need for parents to give guidance.

C

1 Opening: thank for birthday card. Mention 18th birthday meal.

2 Briefly say who was there. Describe what ate – great!

3 One or two paragraphs on what happened:
   eg a Good things: surprise guest and/or present; sang songs/played games
       b Bad things: someone fell ill; family argument

4 Ending: ask about pen friend's 18th birthday.

B Writing

1 When writing your answer you should aim to include various 'ingredients'. Match each writing type **1–3** to the appropriate list of 'ingredients' **a–c**.

1 Informal letter **2** Short story **3** Essay

a • a clear statement of your opinion
   • clear organization and development of ideas
   • formal linking words, eg *In addition, However, Therefore*

b • appropriate opening and closing formulae
   • informal language and expressions
   • informal linking words, eg *and, but, so*

c • a variety of past tenses
   • a wide range of vocabulary (including phrasal verbs)
   • time linkers, eg *as soon as, afterwards, while*

2 Write an answer to one of the questions in Planning above using between **120–180** words. You may follow the relevant plan (**A–C**) or you may write your own. You should aim to include the relevant 'ingredients' from section 1.

For more information on each of the writing types you should look again at the following units.

	Coursebook	Workbook
Essay	3, 8	3, 4, 9
Short story	4, 6	5
Informal letters	1, 9	1, 2, 10
	Ready for writing	

3 Write an answer to one of the questions below. Choose a different writing type to the one you chose in **2**. Don't forget to make a plan before you start to write.

Timing

In the exam you will have approximately 40 minutes to write each answer. Try following these guidelines when writing your answer to the question below:

5 minutes	Make a plan
30 minutes	Write your answer
5 minutes	Check your work

1 You have recently had a class discussion on the subject of fitness and health. Your teacher has asked you to write an essay giving your opinion on the following statement:

People worry too much about fitness and health.

Write your **essay**.

2 You have decided to enter a short-story competition. The competition rules say that the story must begin or end with the words:

My arm hurt so much I felt sure I must have broken it.

Write your **story** for the competition.

3 You recently decided to lead a more healthy lifestyle. Write a letter to your pen friend describing the changes you have made **and** telling him/her what benefits you have noticed so far.

Write your **letter**.

Reading

FCE Part 3

Multiple matching

1 You are going to read an article in which people talk about money. For questions **1–15**, choose from the people (**A–F**). Some of the people may be chosen more than once. When more than one answer is required, these may be given in any order.

Which person or people

have lost friends?	1 ☐	2 ☐
does not want to owe money to anyone?	3 ☐	
are optimistic about the future?	4 ☐	5 ☐
are able to save money for the future?	6 ☐	7 ☐
gives in to pressure?	8 ☐	
inherited some money?	9 ☐	
say that attitudes to money have changed?	10 ☐	11 ☐
mention employment they do not enjoy?	12 ☐	13 ☐
have had to change their lifestyle?	14 ☐	15 ☐

Money makes the world go round?

Steve Mummery talks to six different people about the importance of money in their lives.

A   Reginald I don't have a credit card, I've never taken out a loan and I certainly couldn't ask my friends to lend me money. I suppose it's a generational thing. When I was younger you had to get by on what you'd got, watching every penny to make sure you got to the end of the month. It was unheard of in my family to borrow money. Nowadays, people don't think twice before going into debt to buy a new car or whatever. I have to live on the basic state pension, which isn't very much, yet I still manage to put some money to one side each week, just in case I need it later.

B   Ruth Money's a bit tight at the moment. My husband's out of work and I only work part-time, but we're just about able to make ends meet. Of course, we've had to make a few cuts to adapt to the circumstances. We got rid of the car last month, which has helped enormously, and we've stopped buying new clothes and things. There's no point looking a million dollars if you can't pay the bills. Still, things can only get better and I'm sure we'll sort our situation out, sooner or later.

C   Lester A year ago I was a hard-up student, struggling to survive on a grant. Then my uncle died and I came into quite a large sum of money. I don't have money to burn but I do have enough to make life more comfortable. Unfortunately, one or two so-called friends of mine thought it gave them the right to depend on me to buy them drinks all the time, and they got quite upset when I refused. I'd rather go drinking on my own than have that type of person around me.

D   Trudy I've got a job on Saturdays working in a clothes shop. It's really dull, but I get paid quite well, and that gives me the freedom to do things I couldn't afford to if I had to rely on pocket money from my mum and dad. Of course, I spend some of it on going out with my friends, but I've also opened a savings account; I'd like to have a motorbike by the time I'm 18.

E   Bob I started doing the lottery five years ago, and since then I haven't missed a day. I've only had a couple of small wins, but I feel sure my luck's going to change; the law of averages says it must. I'd do anything to win the jackpot and give up my monotonous job. Any spare money I have is spent on lottery tickets; I've stopped buying records and clothes, and I hardly ever go out now. The fact is, my mates don't bother phoning me up any more, but I don't really mind. I'm prepared to make sacrifices.

F   Alison Our kids seem to think we're made of money. They always want money for this and money for that; computer games, designer clothes, videos and CDs. I'm not saying we didn't want things when we were kids, but at least we had some idea of the value of things. We'd never have dreamed of asking our parents for the sort of amounts our two, and many others like them, do. I'm sure kids these days think money grows on trees. We've tried saying 'no', but I have to confess we don't always succeed.

2   Find words or phrases in the texts which mean the same as the words given below. The letters in brackets refer to the relevant texts.

   1 to save money (A) _____
   2 we don't have much money (B) _____
   3 to get by financially (B) _____
   4 looking very beautiful (B) _____
   5 having very little money (C) _____
   6 inherited (C) _____
   7 have more money than is needed (C) _____
   8 the biggest prize (E) _____
   9 we have a lot of money (F) _____
   10 money is easy to get (F) _____

Vocabulary

Wordlist on page 205 of the Coursebook

A   Money

1   One of the items of vocabulary in each group is not normally used with the word or words in capital letters. Underline the item which does not fit.

Example:
SPEND   *too much*   *a fortune*   <u>*the receipt*</u>   *£2 on sweets*

You can *spend too much, spend a fortune* and *spend £2 on sweets,* but you cannot *spend the receipt.*

1 **PAY**	the rent	change	a fine	tax
2 **PAY BY**	cheque	credit card	debt	direct debit
3 **RATE OF**	interest	inflation	exchange	bill
4 **BUY SOMETHING**	on loan	on credit	on impulse	second-hand
5 owe	open	close	credit	**AN ACCOUNT**
6 bank	savings	coin	current	**ACCOUNT**
7 invest	inherit	do	withdraw	**MONEY**
8 sell	repay	apply for	take out	**A LOAN**

2   Complete the gaps with a word or words that you have underlined in **1** above. The first one has been done for you.

   1 If it isn't the right size, bring it back to the shop with <u>*the receipt*</u> and we'll change it for you.
   2 Could you give me a 10 pence _____ for the phone?
   3 I'm not lending you any more money! You still _____ me £10 from last week.
   4 The paintings by Turner are currently _____ to the Prado Museum. They'll be back here next month.
   5 Have you paid the electricity _____ yet?
   6 **a:** £9.50, please.
      b: Here's £10. Keep the _____ .
   7 I hate being in _____ , which is why I never borrow money from anybody.

B Revision: Lexical phrases

Lexical phrase list on pages 124 and 125

Complete each of the gaps with the correct form of one of the verbs in the box. You will need to use each verb twice. The first one has been done for you.

get	have	take	come	give	put	make	do

1 He cut himself quite badly, so he was _taken_ to hospital, where he was _given_ an anti-tetanus injection.

2 He knew he had _made_ several silly mistakes in the exam, so it _gave_ as no surprise to him to hear that he'd failed. *came*

3 Lubowski, a piano teacher for 42 years, _got_ great pride in the fact that she had _had_ an important influence on the playing styles of some of the world's finest pianists. *having*

4 Recently we've been _had_ a lot of difficulty _making_ our son to _do_ his homework. *doing*

5 I had considered _to do_ research, until I found out just how much time and effort I would need to _come_ into it. *Put*

6 I've _come_ to the conclusion that a lot of these off-piste skiers are just selfish; as well as _put_ their own lives at risk, they endanger those of the rescue services who are called out to help them when they _get_ into trouble. *putting*

7 The director _gave_ a deep sigh when he saw the figures for June; the company had _made_ a loss of £3 million in the first half of the year.

Language focus

 Grammar reference on pages 216 and 217 of the Coursebook

A Ability

In five of the following sentences there is a mistake in the part which is underlined. Find the mistakes and rewrite the sentences so that they are correct.

1 I could dance like that when I was your age. *I was able to*
   I used to dance

2 Trevor could mend the washing machine yesterday; it's working perfectly now. *managed to*

3 I couldn't do the homework last night – it was far too difficult.
   I didn't manage

4 He could hear someone moving about in the kitchen. He went downstairs to investigate. *he was able*

5 I offered to help him but he said he could do it on his own.

6 I've never could swim very well.

7 I don't understand why he's the manager; he's incapable to organize anything. *not skilled at*

8 Did you manage to get in touch with Stephen last night?

9 Jane's very busy, so she won't can come until later.

10 They didn't succeed to get into the final last year; they were beaten 3–1 in the semi-finals. *in ing*

100

B Phrasal verbs and prepositions

Complete each of the gaps with one of the words from the box. You will need to use some words more than once.

off	on	out	round	up	for	of	from

The trip of a lifetime

In a month's time I'll be setting **(1)** _____ on the trip of a lifetime. My plan is to cycle all the way **(2)** _____ the world, starting and finishing in my home town of Plymouth. It's taken over two years to prepare **(3)** _____ the adventure; planning it, training for it and organizing the finance. I've saved **(4)** _____ about a quarter of the money I need, and I've managed to raise the rest by doing **(5)** _____ my house and selling it **(6)** _____ a lot more than it originally cost me. Fortunately, I've received some sponsorship from a bicycle manufacturer, so I haven't had to pay **(7)** _____ the ten replacement bicycles I've calculated I'll need; I've worked **(8)** _____ that at least five will be damaged in accidents and I'll almost certainly be robbed **(9)** _____ another three or four during the trip.

Understandably, my parents are not very keen **(10)** _____ the idea, and I don't blame them **(11)** _____ wanting to try to discourage me **(12)** _____ going. They still haven't forgiven me **(13)** _____ the worry I caused them when I tried, unsuccessfully, to cycle from Norway to South Africa. They've finally accepted, however, that nothing will prevent me **(14)** _____ attempting it, and my mum has said she'll be the first to congratulate me **(15)** _____ my achievement when I get back in two years' time.

Use of English

FCE Part 1

Multiple-choice cloze

For questions **1–12**, decide which answer (**A**, **B**, **C** or **D**) best fits each gap. There is an example at the beginning (**0**).

A success story

At 19, Ben Way was (**0**) _already_ a millionaire, and one of a number of teenagers who (**1**) _M__ their fortune through the Internet. (**2**) _____ makes Ben's story all the more remarkable is that he is dyslexic, and was (**3**) _____ by teachers at his junior school that he would never be able to read or write properly. 'I wanted to prove them (**4**) _____ ,' says Ben, creator and director of Waysearch, a net search engine which can be used to find goods in online shopping malls.

When he was eight, his local authorities (**5**) _____ him with a PC to help with school work. Although he was (**6**) _____ to read the manuals, he had a natural ability with the computer, and encouraged by his father, he soon began (**7**) _____ people £10 an hour for his knowledge and skills. At the age of 15 he (**8**) _____ up his own computer consultancy, Quad Computer, which he ran from his bedroom, and two years later he left school to (**9**) _____ all his time to business.

'By this time the company had grown and I needed to take on a (**10**) _____ of employees to help me,' says Ben. 'That enabled me to start (**11**) _____ business with bigger companies.' It was his ability to consistently (**12**) _____ difficult challenges that led him to win the 'Young Entrepreneur of the Year' award in the same year that he formed Waysearch.

	A	**B**	**C**	**D**
0	yet	just	already	even
1	taken	made	put	done
2	This	That	Something	What
3	said	told	suggested	reported
4	wrong	false	untrue	unfair
5	provided	gave	offered	got
6	impossible	incapable	disabled	unable
7	owing	charging	lending	borrowing
8	put	ran	made	set
9	pay	spend	devote	invest
10	couple	few	little	deal
11	having	doing	making	bringing
12	overcome	overlook	overtake	overdo

FCE Part 3

Word formation

Use the word given in capitals at the end of some of the lines to form a word that fits in the gap **in the same line**. There is an example at the beginning (0).

A narrow escape

Terry Little gave his parents the (0) ___*fright*___ of their lives last   **FRIGHTEN**
weekend when he fell nearly 100 metres down one of the
(1) ___highest___ cliffs in England. Rescue services were   **HIGH**
(2) ___amazed___ , however, when they found Terry lying unconscious,   **AMAZE**
but alive, on the beach below. 'His condition was (3) ___surprisingly___   **SURPRISE**
good,' said one doctor at Penzance General Hospital, where Terry
was taken. His (4) ___injuries___ were limited to a few minor cuts   **INJURE**
and bruises and two (5) ___broken___ teeth. His   **BREAK**
(6) ___survival___ was described as 'a miracle' by his parents, who   **SURVIVE**
had watched in horror and (7) ___disbelief___ as their son was   **BELIEVE**
blown off the cliff by a sudden gust of wind. 'We felt sure
he had fallen to his (8) ___death___ ,' said Terry's father. 'The news   **DIE**
that he was safe and (9) ___reasonably___ well came as an enormous   **REASONABLE**
(10) ___relief___ . We certainly won't be going near any more   **RELIEVE**
cliffs for a while.'

FCE Part 4

Transformations

Complete the second sentence so that it has a similar meaning to the first sentence, using the word given. **Do not change the word given**. You must use between **two** and **five** words, including the word given.

1 We've decided where we're going on holiday.
   UP
   We've ___come up with / made up our minds___ where we're going on holiday.

2 He telephoned several people before lunch.
   CALLS
   He ___gave calls to many people / made several telephone calls___ before lunch.

3 We found it difficult to choose.
   WAS
   It ___was a difficult choice___ for us to make.

4 They can't prove he's guilty.
   NO
   They have ___no proof of / no ways for___ his guilt.

5 The President offered his congratulations to the players when they won the cup.
   CONGRATULATED
   The President ___congratulated the players on winning / on___ the cup.

6 I forgot her birthday last year and she still hasn't forgiven me.
   ME
   She still hasn't forgiven ___me for having forgotten her birthday___ last year.

7 The two sides were unable to reach an agreement.
   SUCCEED
   The two sides ___didn't succeed in reaching___ an agreement.

8 He may be 50, but he can run a marathon in under three hours.
   CAPABLE
   He may be 50, but he ___is capable of running___ a marathon in under three hours.

Writing

FCE Part 2

Reports

See pages 152 and 153 in Unit 12 of the Coursebook for more information on writing reports.

1 Read the following Part 2 question.

A group of elderly tourists will be spending a morning in your town as part of a ten-day tour of the region. The local tourist office has asked you to write a report for the group leader, suggesting ways in which the tourists might spend the morning. You should give advice on sightseeing and shopping, as well as information on where they could have lunch.

Write your **report**.

2 The following report was written in answer to the question above. Put the paragraphs in the correct order and write a suitable heading for each one.

Visit to Roxburgh

1

For those who would rather go shopping, the open-air market in the main square is to be recommended for its wide range of goods, all at bargain prices. The square also includes a number of exclusive gift shops, some of which offer generous discounts to senior citizens.

2

Although the group is only in Roxburgh for a short time, everyone is guaranteed a warm welcome and a memorable morning.

3

Some members of the group might like to begin the morning with a visit to the 16th century church, with its impressive and colourful stained glass windows. Within easy walking distance of the church is the Roxburgh Folk Museum, containing numerous exhibits which show what life was like in the town in former centuries.

4

The aim of this report is to give suggestions to a group of elderly tourists on how best to spend their morning in Roxburgh.

5

After a busy morning the visitors can enjoy a reasonably priced lunch in one of several restaurants on the riverfront. Non-vegetarians should try one of the many fresh fish dishes for which Roxburgh is famous.

Find examples in the model of the following:

Different ways of referring to the tourists eg *Some members of the group*	Different ways of making recommendations eg *might like to begin the morning with*
Words expressing number or quantity eg *Some members*	Words and expressions related to cost eg *all at bargain prices*

3 Writing task

a Read the following writing task.

Some young foreign students are on an exchange programme in your region and are planning to visit your town one day for the afternoon and evening. You have been asked to write a report for the teacher in charge of the group, suggesting ways in which the students might spend their time in your town without having to spend much money. You should give advice on cheap places to go for shopping, entertainment and eating out.

Write your **report**.

Before you write your answer, do the tasks in **b** and **c** below.

b Answer the following questions.
- Who is the target reader of the report?
- Should you write your report in a more formal or informal style?
- What differences do you notice between this task and the one in **1** above?

c Useful vocabulary
The writing task asks you to give advice on cheap places for the students to go to. Put a tick next to those words or expressions below which suggest that something is **not expensive**.

Words to describe prices

| reasonable   exorbitant   inflated   affordable   competitive | PRICES |

Words to describe goods

| cut-price   overpriced   exclusive   inexpensive   luxury | GOODS |

Other words and expressions

| good bargains   discounts   special offers a little on the dear side   good value for money |

4 Now write your report in answer to the task in **3a** above.

Don't forget!

- Divide your report into paragraphs, including a brief introduction and conclusion.
- Give each of your paragraphs a heading.
- You can invent the information in your report if you want to.
- You should not write more than **180** words. Note that each paragraph in the model contains fewer than 55 words.

Reading

FCE Part 2

1 Gapped text

You are going to read an article about a farm animal sanctuary. Seven sentences have been removed from the article. Choose from the sentences **A–H** the one which fits each gap (**1–7**). There is one extra sentence which you do not need to use.

Animal Rescue

Katie Smart visits a remarkable woman who dedicates her life to saving farm animals from cruelty.

In 1990 Carole Webb set up a sanctuary to rescue abandoned or mistreated farm animals. She's so dedicated to the well-being of her animals that they've taken over her income, her life and her heart. Carole lives with her 'family' – some 500 sheep, goats, lambs, calves, pigs and chickens – amongst a jumble of old farm buildings.

The sanctuary is near Fen Drayton, in a remote area to the west of Cambridge. Surrounded by acres of flat land, without so much as a tree in sight, it seems cut off from the rest of humanity. Carole's nearest neighbours are two miles away and she often goes days at a time without speaking to another person. **1** 'When I was a little girl I always spent more time with my pets and I could never bear to see any of them suffer. The animals that arrive here are frightened and in a state of shock,' she explains. 'But they soon change, with love and care. Animals that are often considered stupid show remarkable intelligence once they've got over their fear.'

Inspiration for the sanctuary came when Carole, who trained as a veterinary nurse, was living in Hertfordshire. **2** 'One day I noticed that one of them had a broken leg. I told the farmer and asked him if he needed any help looking after sick animals. Within a couple of years I'd bought this place and set up my own sanctuary.'

When Carole first moved in, she inherited some 15 sheep from the farmer. **3** 'When I found him he was cold, hungry and close to death,' she recalls. 'I bottle-fed him, wrapped him up warmly next to the kitchen fire and nursed him back to health.' He is still alive and well, although he's getting a little bad tempered and prefers people not to go near him.

4 He's always on the hunt for cakes and biscuits and he won't leave you alone until he's made sure you're not hiding one behind your back. It's hard to believe when you see the size of him that he was found abandoned by the side of a road – cold, weak and hungry. Now he's very much the boss in the sanctuary, and expects to be treated like a VIP, or 'very important pig'.

In Carole's eyes all her animals have their own personalities, and if they could speak, all would have an alarming story to tell. **5** Carole rescued her and three days later Gismo the lamb was born.

Then there's Gromit the Friesian cow who was left to die because the farmer couldn't pay his vet's bills, or Petal the goat who suffered terribly for over a year. She had a broken leg and her owners were supposed to take her back to the vet within a few months so that he could take her plaster cast off. **6** 'The poor animal was in agony,' Carole tells me. 'The vet refused to let them take her home again. Instead, he gave her to me to take care of. It's amazing she lets anyone go near her after the treatment she received, but she's very happy and loves being with people.'

The sanctuary's survival is constantly at risk. **7** 'I remember crying to my friend on the phone, thinking that we'd have to close down. It was she who came up with the idea of starting up an adoption scheme,' explains Carole. 'Over 400 people have now sponsored an animal, and we have about 40 life members, all of whom have paid money to help keep the sanctuary going.'

A Wiggy the pig, on the other hand, is difficult to get rid of.

B Some of the animals arrive in a terrible condition, but at Carole's Farm Animal Sanctuary they all have a future.

C Carole openly confesses to preferring the company of animals to humans.

D It costs Carole £600 a week for hay and animal food, and the vet's bill can be as much as £1,000 a month.

E One of them was Larry the lamb, whose mother died soon after his birth.

F Take the sheep who was destined for the butcher's, despite being in an advanced state of pregnancy.

G She had a pony, which she kept in a field, and she would often go to the nearby farm to watch the lambs.

H But they didn't return until 15 months later.

2 Find phrasal verbs in the main part of the text which have the following meanings.

1 establish or start
(a new organization or business) _____
2 take control of _____
3 separate or isolate _____
4 recover from _____
5 take care of _____
6 think of and suggest (an idea) _____

3 Write the noun form of each of the following words. All the nouns appear in the text.

Adjective	Noun
cruel	_____
pregnant	_____
intelligent	_____
healthy	_____

Verb	Noun
treat	_____
adopt	_____
survive	_____
inspire	_____

Vocabulary

Wordlist on page 205 of the Coursebook

A Crossword: The Arts

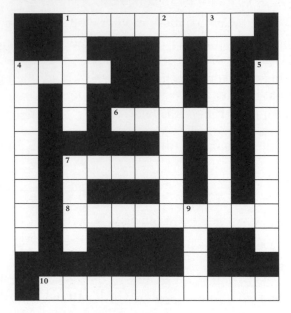

Across

1 a person who creates objects out of materials such as wood, stone or metal
4 you go to the theatre to see one
6 Romeo dies in the third _____ of Act V of Shakespeare's play *Romeo and Juliet*.
7 operas are performed in an opera _____
8 a painting showing a view of the countryside
10 you go to an art gallery to see an _____ of paintings

Down

1 the area in a theatre on which the actors perform
2 adjective to describe a painting or other object which is extremely valuable
3 a large group of musicians who play many different instruments together
4 a painting of a person
5 a person who writes music, especially classical music
7 a concert _____ is a place where concerts are given
9 collective noun for actors in 4 across

B Phrasal verbs: Revision

Phrasal verbs with more than one meaning

1 Use the following verbs and particles to make phrasal verbs which have both, or all three meanings, in each group **a–f**.

Example: *fall for*
fall in love with (someone)
be deceived by (a trick)

| do | get | take |
| make | put | fall |

| out | off | with |
| up | on | for |

a *take up*
accept (a challenge/an offer)
start doing (a new sport/hobby)
use or occupy (time or space)

b *Put off*
postpone (an event)
distract someone
discourage someone

c *do up*
fasten or button up (clothes)
repair or redecorate (a room/a building)

d *make out*
pretend or claim falsely that something is true
see hear or understand something with difficulty

e *get on with*
have a good relationship with someone
start or continue doing (work/a job)

f *make up*
invent (a story/an excuse)
become friends again (after an argument)

g *put up*
accommodate someone (in your house/flat)
increase (prices)

2 Complete each of the gaps with the correct form of one of the phrasal verbs in **1**.

1 I must have put on weight – I can't ___put on___ these trousers any more.
2 Stop talking everyone and ___get on with___ your work!
3 She decided to get rid of some her books; they were ___taking up___ too much room in her flat.
4 He ___made out___ that he'd written the poem himself, but we all thought he must have copied it from a book.
5 I wanted to see that opera, but I was ___put off___ by the cost of the tickets.
6 We often have arguments and fall out, but it's never very long before we kiss and ___make up___ again.
7 The only way to stop people using their cars is by ___putting up___ the price of petrol.
8 He told me I'd spilt something on my jacket, but I didn't _____ that old trick. I knew he was after my wallet.

Language focus

(G) Grammar reference on page 217 of the Coursebook

1 Complete the gaps with the correct form of the verb in brackets.

1 I wish we ___had___ (have) more time to do the homework. I won't be able to finish it by tomorrow.
2 I wish you ___wouldn't make___ (not/make) so much noise. I'm trying to concentrate.
3 The water in that river looks wonderful. If only I ___had brought___ (bring) my swimming costume.
4 The photocopier's broken down again. I wish I ___knew___ (know) how to fix it.
5 I wish it ___would stop___ (stop) raining. I want to go to the shops.
6 I'd rather you ___didn't tell___ (not/tell) anyone about it yet.
7 My wife wants to go to Italy on holiday, but I'd rather ___go___ (go) to Spain.
8 It's time I ___bought___ (buy) some new shoes. These ones have got holes in them.

2 What would you say in each of the following situations? Complete the sentences. The first one has been done for you.

1 Your exams are in two weeks' time and you haven't done any revision yet.
It's high time I _started revising for my exams_ .
2 Your classmate hasn't got a watch and is always asking you what time it is.
It's about time you ___got a watch / bought___ .
3 Your friend wants to come and see you at 8 o'clock, but there's a good film on TV which starts at 7:30.
I'd rather you ___didn't come at 8... come around after the film has finished___ .
4 You're trying to tell your brother something but he keeps interrupting.
I wish you ___would not interrupt me – stop interrupting me___ .
5 Your FCE exam is on Saturday so you won't be able to watch your favourite team play in the cup final.
I wish ___the FCE exam weren't on Satur / were on a different day___ .
6 Someone stole your video camera on holiday. It wasn't insured.
If only ___my camera would be insured / I'd insured the video___ .
7 You have been waiting nearly 30 minutes for your bus to come.
I wish ___the bus would come – I'd caught the train___ .
8 You have just got back from holiday to find that all your houseplants have died.
If only ___I had / I'd got smn to water the plants___ .

Use of English

FCE Part 3

Word formation

Use the word given in capitals at the end of some of the lines to form a word that fits in the gap **in the same line**. There is an example at the beginning **(0)**.

Modern art

Modern art has become rather **(0)** _fashionable_ in the North-East   **FASHION**
of England, and large metallic **(1)** _sculptures_ are now fairly   **SCULPT**
commonplace in the region. The **(2)** _____ known of   **WELL**
these is the 200-ton steel figure, Angel of the North, erected in
Gateshead at the **(3)** _____ cost of £800,000. Many local   **CONSIDER**
people were horrified at the **(4)** _____ to spend such a large   **DECIDE**
sum on a 65-foot metal structure. Nevertheless, the Angel is
(5) _possibly_ one of the most frequently viewed artworks in   **POSSIBLE**
the world, seen **(6)** _daily_ by almost 100,000 passing motorists.   **DAY**
A number of **(7)** _residents_ in Hartlepool were similarly upset   **RESIDE**
when they were greeted one day by the **(8)** _sight_ of 15   **SEE**
giant, metal balls on a traffic roundabout in the town centre.
They described the payment of £70,000 for the spheres as
(9) _____ and felt the money could have been spent on   **RESPONSIBLE**
something more directly **(10)** _____ to the local population.   **BENEFIT**

FCE Part 2

Open cloze

Read the text below and think of the word which best fits each gap. Use only **one** word in each gap. There is an example at the beginning **(0)**.

Animal mummies

Over the centuries millions of animal mummies **(0)** _have_ been discovered in
Egypt, **(1)** _____ lying alongside human mummies, and others in their own separate
cemeteries. We know, of course, that the Egyptians mummified pharaohs, queens and
priests to ensure **(2)** _their_ passage into the afterlife. But why did they bury so
(3) _____ animals?

Some, **(4)** _it_ seems, were pets; in the same way that possessions were buried
(5) _____ the use of the dead in the afterlife, a favourite cat, dog or monkey would
(6) _be_ sacrificed in order to keep the deceased company there. Other animals,
however, were intended **(7)** _as_ gifts to the gods; a crocodile to please Sobek
or a cow for Hathor. Whole catacombs were dedicated to particular animals, such
as cats, dogs or birds, **(8)** _that_ were buried in large numbers, possibly to mark
a religious festival. **(9)** _____ animal was considered too small or insignificant
for mummification: snakes, beetles, fish of all sizes and even the eggs of birds and
reptiles.

(10) _____ animal mummies were clearly very important to the ancient Egyptians,
few studies have been carried out on the subject, perhaps because **(11)** _____ has
always been more interest **(12)** _____ human mummies.

FCE Part 4 — Transformations

For questions **1–6**, complete the second sentence so that it has a similar meaning to the first sentence, using the word given. **Do not change the word given.** You must use between **two** and **five** words, including the word given.

1 We were very impressed by how generous he was.
US
His _generosity impressed us so /very_ much.

2 He hasn't fully recovered yet.
FULL
He hasn't made _a full recovery_ yet.

3 We couldn't choose where we sat in the classroom.
HAD
We _had no choice (about)_ we sat in the classroom.

4 Although the bus arrived late, we managed to get there on time.
DESPITE
We managed to get there on time, _despite of the delay_ the bus.
the late arrival of / the lateness of

5 'I do not intend to resign,' said the President.
INTENTION
The President said _he had no intention of_ resigning.
has

6 I am not sure exactly how deep the harbour is.
EXACT
I am not sure _about / the exact depth_ of the harbour.
_of_

Writing

FCE Paper 2

Read the Paper 2 Writing questions below. Before you write any answers, do the preparation exercises on page 113.

Part 1 You **must** answer this question.

1 You have received an email from your penfriend, Richard, whose parents are planning to visit your area for two days. Read Richard's email and the notes you have made. Then, write an email to Richard, using **all** your notes.

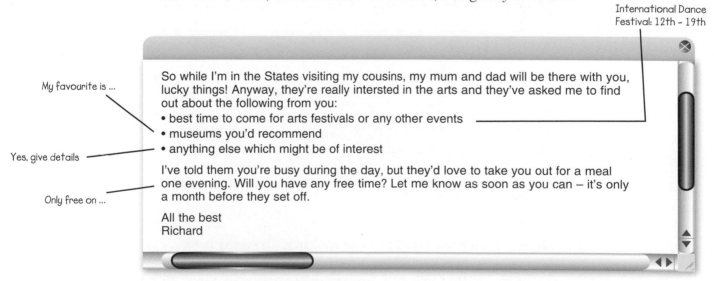

International Dance Festival: 12th – 19th

My favourite is …

Yes, give details

Only free on …

So while I'm in the States visiting my cousins, my mum and dad will be there with you, lucky things! Anyway, they're really intersted in the arts and they've asked me to find out about the following from you:
• best time to come for arts festivals or any other events
• museums you'd recommend
• anything else which might be of interest

I've told them you're busy during the day, but they'd love to take you out for a meal one evening. Will you have any free time? Let me know as soon as you can – it's only a month before they set off.

All the best
Richard

Write your **email** in **120–150** words. You must use grammatically correct sentences with accurate spelling and punctuation in a style appropriate for the situation.

Part 2 Write an answer to **one** of the questions 2–5 in this part. Write your answer in
120–180 words in an appropriate style.

2 You are studying in England for a year and you see the following advertisement in
a local newspaper:

> **PET SHOP**
> requires a part-time shop assistant for three months.
> Duties include: feeding and caring for pets, serving in shop, advising customers
> on animal care.
> • love and knowledge of animals essential
> • previous experience of shop work preferred
> Foreign students welcome: must have reasonable level of spoken English
> *Contact: Mr P Sayers, Pet Paradise, 38 Portland Road, Hove BN41 6JF*

Write your **letter of application** to Mr Sayers, asking for more information about
the working hours and pay.

3 Your town has been given a large sum of money to be spent on **either** a zoo **or** a
concert hall. Write a report for the town council describing the benefits to the town
of both proposals and say which one you think the money should be spent on.

Write your **report**.

4 You see the following advertisement in a magazine for pet lovers.

> **Writing Competition**
> We would like to receive your articles with the following title:
> **MY SPECIAL FRIEND**
> Write to us about your pet, telling our readers how it came to be in your family
> and what makes it so special.
> The writer of the best entry will receive a year's supply of food for their pet.

Write your **article** for the writing competition.

5 Answer **one** of the following two questions on **one** of the set books you have read.

a If you have seen a film version of the book write a review of the film for your
school's English-language magazine. Tell readers how the film differs from the book
and in what ways it is similar. You should also say whether you prefer the film or
the book and why.

Write your **review**.

b You have been asked to write an article about the book for the school's English-
language magazine. They would like you to imagine which actors you would choose
to play **two** of the main characters in the book, if a new film version were made.
Give reasons for your choices.

Write your **article**.

Preparation for Part 1

Remember that candidates who write good answers to Part 1 questions attempt to build on the information given by adding relevant points of their own.

In order to prepare for the Part 1 question on page 111, decide first what extra information you could give. Make notes for each of the following:

International Dance Festival	*What type of dance is performed (eg modern, classical, folk etc)?* *Which countries participate?*
Museum	*What type of exhibits are on display?* *Why would you recommend it?*
Something else of interest	*What is it and why might it be of interest to Richard's parents? (eg another museum, concert, sculpture park etc)*
Going out for a meal	*Why are you only free on the particular day(s) you mention?*

Don't forget!

You should not write more than **150** words, so you may not be able to include **all** this extra information.

Language preparation

a In **1–10** below complete each of the gaps with one of the phrases from the box.

that struck me	have no experience of	I like most about her
obvious choice	sum up	main difference	express an interest
aim of this report	looking forward to	pleased to hear

1 The _____ is to consider the benefits of ...

2 I'm really _____ meeting them.

3 Although I _____ working in a pet shop, I spent the last two summers helping my uncle in his newsagent's.

4 The first thing _____ about her was her lovely smooth fur.

5 I was _____ your parents are coming.

6 To _____ , I recommend that the money should be spent on the zoo, mainly because ...

7 What _____ is her lively nature and almost limitless energy.

8 I am writing to _____ in the job I saw advertised in the York Gazette.

9 His good looks and deep voice would make him the _____ for the role.

10 The _____ , of course, is the historical period in which each is set.

b In answer to which question is each sentence written?
eg *Sentence 1, Question 3*

Writing task

Write an answer to the Part 1 question. Then choose one of the Part 2 questions and write an answer.

For more information on each of the writing types you should look again at the following units.

Task type	Coursebook	Workbook
Informal letters and emails	1, 9, Ready for writing	1, 2, 10
Letter of application	5	6
Report	12	13
Article	2, 10	3, 11
Review	4	7

Reading

Multiple choice

1 You are going to read a newspaper article about body language. For questions **1–8**, choose the answer (**A, B, C** or **D**) which you think fits best according to the text.

The truth behind body language

Non-verbal actions can tell different – and more genuine – messages than words, discovers Karen Hainsworth

Words convey the messages that we want others to hear, but our bodies may tell a different story. Whether we express our problems to our colleagues with a hunched back and sad, downcast eyes, or our enthusiasm for life with a cheerful spring in our step, our bodies are constantly sending out messages. And understanding these clues that we unavoidably offer each other is an essential part of effective communication.

'People vary enormously in their ability to detect non-verbal cues,' says Dr Peter Bull, psychologist at University of York. 'Those who tend to be good at detecting emotions and getting the timing right when raising tricky subjects are usually picking up others' moods through these non-verbal clues,' he says. 'But it's important to be emotionally intelligent when dealing with the real messages that are coming through. There's little point in being a skilled decoder of subtle signals if your colleagues' more genuine emotions overwhelm you with anxiety, anger or irritation.'

The ability to manipulate your own body language is suggested as an essential skill when it comes to making a good impression. 'If you're aiming to communicate interest and enthusiasm at an interview, for example, confident body language can help to convey a message that is consistent,' says Bull. 'General facial cues suggesting alertness, while showing that you are listening, can help. And your tone of voice should be lively and interested.'

Though we can portray a false emotion to a certain extent, few can fool a skilled observer, who is likely to detect the micro-expressions that we constantly make. We may smile when we are miserable, but a body-
line 37 language expert will know we're faking it. Genuine smiles use the tiny muscles around the eyes, but a false smile involves only the mouth.

It's not that difficult to modify grosser signals, however. And we can make a good start by developing a level of self-awareness. 'It's important to listen to what our own bodies are doing,' says Dr Betty Rudd, the chartered counselling psychologist.

'We might not recognize what we're feeling, but if we note our crossed arms and tense posture suddenly, we recognize that we're defensive and anxious. And so we might be saying the right words to someone but our body is saying "go away".'

If you want to give the impression of confidence at work, first recognize how much space you are taking up. 'Think about letting go of the tension in your muscles; allow the floor or the chair to take their weight,' says Rudd. 'Think of your back spreading out and widening and lengthening.' And she suggests maintaining eye contact with the person you are dealing with, rather than constantly averting your gaze. 'These little things can make a huge impact and you will feel more grounded and secure,' she says.

But most of us are so busy doing our jobs that we fail to take any notice what our bodies are doing. Rudd says: 'Become aware of how you are sitting or standing. If someone was looking at you, what would they think you were feeling? You can change your posture and the message you are giving by setting yourself little reminders. For example, you might say to yourself, "Every time I see a bus, I'm going to stop and look at my body and note what I am thinking and question whether this is how I want to be".'

Once you become aware of these subtle signs, you increase your power to communicate effectively. When your body is saying the same thing as your words, it shows consistency or congruence and that has enormous impact. But people will often use incongruence to get less comfortable information across. 'They may say something that makes them sound quite interested in you, but their body language suggests they are not,' says Bull. 'They may feel they cannot come out and say, "I'm not interested", so what they do is say it through a lukewarm, uninterested non-verbal style.'

Decoding the real message can be a tricky business and becomes even more complicated when different cultures begin to mix. But whether that's the culture of a country or company, you can avoid putting your foot in it by watching others closely and observing the subtleties of non-verbal cues, while noting the unspoken messages that accompany the words.

1 In the first paragraph we are told that
  A it is inadvisable to express our true feelings through our posture.
  B the words we speak are inconsistent with the gestures we make.
  C a correct interpretation of body language is important for communication.
  D our body is the only true indicator of meaning.

2 Dr Bull says that an understanding of body language needs to be accompanied by
  A a suitable emotional response.
  B an ability to talk about difficult topics.
  C a tendency to express one's emotions.
  D an appropriately high level of intelligence.

3 In an interview situation, Dr Bull says it is important to
  A be more attentive than usual.
  B ensure your whole face is visible.
  C speak in a high-pitched voice.
  D use appropriate body language.

4 What is meant by 'we're faking it' in line 37?
  A we are incapable of laughing
  B we are making fun of others
  C we are trying to cheer ourselves up
  D we are pretending to be happier than we really are

5 The first step to changing more negative aspects of our own body language is to
  A consult a professional psychologist.
  B acknowledge our true feelings.
  C become conscious of our behaviour.
  D attempt to relax more.

6 What does Dr Rudd say to people who want to appear confident?
  A Spread out your whole body to occupy a large space.
  B Adopt a casual posture when standing or sitting.
  C Avoid looking away from people you are talking to.
  D Imagine you are sitting or lying down.

7 What is the purpose of Dr Rudd's example of the bus?
  A to draw a comparison between buses and body language
  B to demonstrate how we can remember to observe ourselves
  C to remind us of the need to sit correctly when travelling by bus
  D to encourage us to compare our posture with that of other passengers

8 According to Dr Bull, some people use body language
  A to express what they dare not say openly.
  B to show how uncomfortable they feel.
  C to hide their true feelings for someone.
  D to conform to the rules of their culture.

2 Write the noun form of each of the words on the left. All these nouns appear in the reading text. There is an example at the beginning (**0**).

0	enthusiastic	*enthusiasm*
1	communicate	_____
2	anxious	_____
3	angry	_____
4	irritate	_____
5	able	_____
6	alert	_____
7	self-aware	_____
8	confident	_____
9	weigh	_____
10	subtle	_____

3 Now write the noun form of the following words. You will need to use the same suffixes as those in **2**.

0	optimistic	*optimism*
1	weak	_____
2	various	_____
3	credible	_____
4	certain	_____
5	persistent	_____
6	complicate	_____
7	complain	_____
8	hungry	_____

Vocabulary

Wordlist on Page 205 of the Coursebook

A Word grid: Education

Use the clues to help you complete the grid with words related to education. When you have all the answers you will find an extra item of vocabulary for number 10 down.

1 children in Britain go to _____ school between the ages of 5 and 11, before they go to secondary school

2 to take an exam again

3 the _____ University offers programmes on the radio and television for students who want to study for a degree at home

4 you can either pass an exam or _____ it

5 an FE college is a college of further _____ for people older than school age

6 maths, history and science are all school _____

7 a _____ school is controlled by the government or local authority. Children do not have to pay to attend

8 _____ and Cambridge are the most famous universities in Britain

9 to study something again in order to prepare for an examination

10 the most senior teacher in a British university department

B Phrasal verbs with *turn*

Phrasal verb list on page 123

Complete each of the gaps with one of the following particles.

off	up	into	on	down	out

1 They offered her the job but she turned it _____ because the salary was so low.

2 I was furious! We arranged to meet at 6 o'clock, but he didn't turn _____ until 7.

3 This building was a dance hall before they turned it _____ a cinema.

4 As soon as he gets up, he turns _____ the television and spends the next three hours watching the cartoons.

5 We got talking, and it turned _____ that we both went to the same school.

6 We've gone too far. We should have turned _____ this road at the last set of traffic lights.

C Expressions with *turn*

Match each of the sentences on the left with one on the right.
Example: 1 c

1 My great-grandfather's over 100 years old.
2 My mum's feeling a little depressed.
3 She looked extremely cold.
4 Let's check the homework.
5 I'm sure she knew we'd been smoking.
6 I did the washing up yesterday.
7 She helped me so I'll help her.
8 She rushed to the hospital to be with him.

a Her face and hands had turned blue.
b Turn to page 42, everyone.
c He was born at the turn of the last century.
d One good turn deserves another.
e She's just turned 40.
f His condition had taken a turn for the worse.
g It's your turn to do it today.
h She seemed to turn a blind eye to it, though.

D Compound adjectives

Form compound adjectives to describe the following.

1 a doctor who received his training in Britain *a British-trained doctor*
2 a car which they make in Spain
3 a guide who speaks Russian
4 a company which has its base in London
5 a supermarket chain whose owners are French
6 a cruise lasting ten days
7 a woman who is 29
8 a book with 650 pages
9 a film lasting four hours
10 a conference from 26th to 28th March inclusive

Language focus

Expressing purpose

1 The following sentences tell a story about Yolanda. Match each of the actions on the left with a reason on the right.
Example: 1 c

Action

1 Yolanda went to Dublin last month.
2 She went on her own, without her Spanish friends.
3 She took a lot of warm clothes.
4 Her host family had learnt a few words of Spanish.
5 Yolanda hired a car when she was there.
6 She bought a couple of guidebooks.
7 She phoned home a few times.
8 She's just signed up for an English course in Madrid.
9 She has kept all her maps and guidebooks.

Reason

a She thought it might be cold there.
b She didn't want her parents to worry about her.
c She wanted to study English.
d She might decide to go back to Ireland next year.
e She didn't want to speak any Spanish.
f She might not have understood any English.
g She doesn't want to forget everything she learnt.
h She wanted to see the rest of the country.
i She wanted to be able to read about the different places before visiting them.

117

2 Join each pair of sentences from exercise **1** using one of the following expressions of purpose. Make any other changes which are necessary.

| in case | so that | so as | (not) to | in order | (not) to |

1 *Yolanda went to Dublin last month in order to study English.*

2 _____

3 _____

4 _____

5 _____

6 _____

7 _____

8 _____

9 _____

Use of English

FCE Part 4

Transformations: Grammar revision

Each of the following transformations revises a different item of grammar from the Coursebook.

Complete the second sentence so that it has a similar meaning to the first sentence, using the word given. **Do not change the word given.** You must use between **two** and **five** words, including the word given.

A Units 1–5

1 I think I'll always find it strange living in a village.
USED
I don't think I'll ever _get used to living_ in a village.

2 I don't really want to go to the park.
FEEL
I don't really _feel like going_ to the park.

3 What time does the film start this evening?
FILM
Do you know what _time the film starts_ this evening?

4 He's a better singer than me.
SING
I can't _sing better than he_ can.

5 His English was so good I didn't realize he was French.
SUCH
He spoke _such good English that_ I didn't realize he was French.

6 Don't tell your mum where we've been.
BETTER
You _had better not tell_ your mum where we've been.

7 We're not allowed to wear trainers to school.
LET
The teachers _don't let us wear_ trainers to school.

B Units 6–9

1 She's too young to appreciate that type of humour.
OLD
She's ___so old that she doesn't___ appreciate that type of humour.

2 We got someone to paint the house last month.
HAD
We ___had the house painted___ last month.

3 Despite the heavy rain, the concert went ahead as planned.
RAINING
Although ___it was raining___ , the concert went ahead as planned.

4 I'd rather watch than play, if you don't mind.
RATHER
I'd prefer ___watch rather than play___ , if you don't mind.

5 I've never seen this group play live before.
TIME
This is the ___first time I see___ this group play live.

6 They probably won't get here on time.
LIKELY
They ___are not likely being to get___ here on time.

7 It's possible that the neighbours saw someone leaving the house.
MIGHT
The neighbours ___might have seen___ someone leaving the house.

C Units 10–15

1 He thought the police were following him.
HE
He thought ___he was followed by___ the police.

2 They say he's making a good recovery in hospital.
SAID
He ___is said he's to be___ making a good recovery in hospital.

3 We missed the plane because our car broke down on the motorway.
NOT
If our car ___had not broken down___ on the motorway, we would
have caught the plane.

4 'Have you been behaving yourself?' Samantha asked her young son.
HE
Samantha asked her young son ___if he had been behaving___ himself.

5 'Would you like me to carry your bags, mother?' asked Jim.
OFFERED
Jim ___offered her mother to carry the___ bags for her.

6 He wasn't able to complete the marathon.
SUCCEED
He ___didn't succeed in completing___ the marathon.

7 I regret spending so much money on the car.
NOT
I wish ___I had not spend___ so much money on the car.

8 He wore an extra jumper because he didn't want to get cold.
SO
He wore an extra jumper ___so he would___ get cold.

FCE Part 2

Open cloze

Read the text below and think of the word which best fits each gap. Use only **one** word in each gap. There is an example at the beginning (**0**).

Greek societies

When young Americans go to university (**0**) __at__ the age of 18, one of the first things many of them do (**1**) _is_ join a fraternity or a sorority, social organizations for male and female students respectively. (**2**) _That~~every~~_ organization uses a combination of letters of the Greek alphabet as its name, such as ADP (Alpha Delta Pi) or GFS (Gamma Phi Sigma). Both fraternities and sororities have (**3**) _their_ own clubhouses, known as 'fraternity houses' or 'sorority houses', (**4**) _~~all~~ where_ members can relax, socialize and give parties.

In (**5**) _order_ to become a member of a society, students (**6**) _have_ to go through a rather lengthy procedure called 'rush'. As part of rush, new students, or 'rushees', visit the different houses (**7**) _so_ that they can find out about each fraternity or sorority and decide which one they (**8**) _would_ most like to join. A rushee may then receive a 'bid', a formal, written invitation from (**9**) _a_ particular fraternity or sorority to become a member of their organization. (**10**) _if_ the rushee likes the organization and decides to accept the bid, then he or she becomes a 'pledge' for a period of time. During (**11**) _that ~~this~~_ period, pledges are made to complete a number of monotonous, and sometimes unpleasant tasks so as (**12**) _~~of they~~_ prove they are worthy of being members of the society.
_to_

FCE Part 3

Word formation

Use the word given in capitals at the end of some of the lines to form a word that fits in the gap **in the same line**. There is an example at the beginning (**0**).

Saving languages

Linguist Jan Enkelmann's mission is to save as many (**0**) _endangered_ **DANGER**
languages as possible. He often goes to some of the most
accessible
inaccessible (**1**) ~~accessful~~ parts of the earth to make detailed **ACCESS**
(**2**) _written_ records of such languages. The work can be difficult **WRITE**
and at times dangerous as some tribes are deeply (**3**) _suspicious_ **SUSPICION**
of language (**4**) _researchers_ like Professor Enkelmann who ask **RESEARCH**
them so many questions. Some linguists have been (**5**) _prisoned_ **PRISON**
or threatened with guns while working in countries where the
(**6**) _political_ situation is unstable. According to Enkelmann, **POLITICS**
olis. the (**7**) _~~appearance~~_ of a language begins when the younger **APPEAR**
generation no longer uses it. And when there are (**8**) _~~less~~ fewer_ **FEW**
than 40 speakers, the language is (**9**) _unlikely_ **LIKELY**
to survive. 'If we
can document a language before it becomes extinct we can help
to preserve the (**10**) _knowledge_ which is possessed by the people **KNOW**
who speak it,' explains Enkelmann.

Writing

FCE Part 1

Formal letters

Read the following Part 1 question.

You have decided to spend two weeks in August studying English in England. You have seen the advertisement below in an international magazine, and you would like to have more details. Using the notes you have made, write to Coastline Language School giving details of your level and specific needs **and** asking for further information.

Study English this summer at
COASTLINE LANGUAGE SCHOOL
on one of our
Summer Intensive Courses

- 20 lessons a week
- £400 for 2 weeks
- £160 per week for host family accommodation
- fully qualified teachers
- friendly atmosphere
- self-study facilities
- computer room
- well-equipped classrooms
- relaxation area
- full social programme
- student card
- easy access to beach and town centre
- accommodation in private houses (includes breakfast & evening meal)

For more details write to: *Coastline Language School, 23 Marine Parade, Worthing BN11 9TP*

for example? I particularly need ...

close to school?

other students in same house?

- My level is ...
- I particularly want to improve my ...

Write your **letter** in **120–150 words** in an appropriate style. Do not write any postal addresses.

Before you write

- Read the section on formal letters in Unit 2 of the Coursebook.
- Look again at page 206 of the Grammar reference for information on indirect questions.

Phrasal verb list

The Coursebook unit(s) in which the phrasal verb occurs is represented by the number(s) in brackets.

Verbs marked with an asterisk*
With these verbs the noun is usually used after the particle. The pronoun, however, must be used before the particle.

Phrasal verb	Meaning
blow something up (9)	destroy something with an explosion
break down (4)	stop working
bring a child up (6)	raise
call for something (12)	demand, request
carry on with something (5)	continue doing
catch on	become popular
catch up on something	spend time doing an activity you have not had time to do recently
cheer someone/yourself up (1/7)	make someone/yourself feel happier
come across something (7/14)	encounter/find by chance
come down with an illness (7)	get an illness
come into money	inherit
come round (7)	come to your house
come up (7)	be mentioned or discussed; arise or appear (in a class/an exam/a meeting)
come up with an idea (7)	think of and suggest an idea
cut down on something	reduce the amount you drink/eat etc
cut something or someone off	separate or isolate
cut something out (15)	stop doing/eating etc something
do away with something (15)	get rid of/destroy
do something up (13/14)	a) fasten, button up clothes
	b) repair, redecorate or modernize a building or room
could do with something (13)	need, would like
couldn't do without something (13)	need something in order to survive or perform a job or task
dress up as something/someone (9)	put on different clothes in order to disguise yourself
*eat up time/money (14)	use or consume in great quantities
fall for a trick	be deceived by

Phrasal verb	Meaning
fall for someone (6)	fall in love with
fall out with someone (6)	argue with someone and stop being friendly with them
find something out (10)	discover
fit a building out (8)	provide with everything that will be needed
get away (for the weekend) (1)	go away for a period of time for a break/a holiday
get away from someone/a place	escape
get away with something (10)	not be punished for doing something
get round someone (10)	persuade someone to allow you to do something by charming them
get someone down (1)	make unhappy/depress
get by (1/14)	manage to survive/live
get on with someone (6)	have a good relationship with
get on with something (14)	start or continue doing something (especially work)
get over something (1)	recover from
get over someone (6)	recover after the end of a relationship with someone
get through something (14)	manage to survive a difficult experience or period of time
get up to something (6)	do things you know you shouldn't
give someone away (9)	show someone's true nature or identity
give secrets away (9)	reveal
give something back to someone (9)	return something to someone
give homework in (9)	hand to the teacher
give in (to someone's requests) (9)	agree to something you do not want to
*give off a smell (9)	produce and send into the air
*give out information (9)	announce or broadcast information
*give paper, books out (9)	distribute to a group of people
give something up (5/9/14)	stop doing
go in for something	do something as a hobby or interest

go out with someone (6)	have a romantic relationship with someone	put posters up (11)	fix to a wall or a board
grow up (6)	slowly become an adult	put someone up for the night (11)	accommodate
hand something out (4)	give something to everyone in a group	put up with someone/ something (8)	tolerate
hang out with someone (10)	spend time with someone, doing nothing in particular	run out of something (10)	use up (eg money, petrol, time)
head for a place (8)	go towards	set off (4/11)	start a journey
hold someone back (5)	prevent someone from making progress	set a company up (5/13)	establish/start
let someone down (6)	disappoint	show off (10)	try to impress people by telling or showing them what you are capable of
let someone off (10)	give someone a lighter punishment than they expected (or not punish at all)	sign up for something	sign a document showing your intention to do something (eg a course)
look after someone (1)	take care of	splash out on something (7)	buy something expensive
look for something (5)	try to find	split up with someone (6)	end a relationship with
look forward to something (1)	feel happy about something that is going to happen	take after someone (4)	resemble a member of your family in appearance, behaviour or character
look into something (10)	investigate	take homework/books in (4)	collect from students
look up to someone (6)	admire and respect	take someone in (10)	trick or deceive someone
make something out (9/13)	see, hear or understand someone/something with difficulty	take someone on (4)	employ
		take over from someone (4)	replace, take responsibility from someone
make out (13)	pretend, claim falsely that something is true	take something over (14)	take control of
make up for something (8/9)	compensate for	take to someone/ something (4)	start to like, especially after only a short time
make something up (10/13)	invent	*take up a challenge/an offer (14)	accept
make (it) up (13)	become friends again	*take up a new sport/hobby (2/4)	start doing
move on (5)	change to a different job, activity or place	*take up time/space (4/14)	use, fill or occupy
move out	stop living in a house or flat	tell someone off (6)	speak angrily to someone who has done something wrong
own up to something (10)	admit to doing something		
pass out (2)	lose consciousness	throw something away (14)	get rid of something you do not need any more
pick someone up (10)	meet/collect someone (eg at the station/from school)	turn back (15)	return towards the place you started from
pull up (4)	slow down and stop	turn someone/something down (15)	reject or refuse
put money aside (11)	save money for a future occasion	turn (something) into (15) something	(cause something to) become something different
*put forward a plan/ explanation/proposal (11)	suggest for consideration	turn off (a road) (15)	leave one road in order to continue on another
put an event off (11)	postpone	turn something off (15)	to disconnect
put someone off (11)	distract	turn something on	to connect
put someone off doing something (11)	discourage	turn out (15)	be discovered/become known
put someone off someone else (11)	cause to dislike	turn something out (15)	to disconnect
put clothes on (1/11)	place on your body	turn up (15)	arrive, usually unexpectedly, early or late
put the radio/TV on (11)	start something working	use something up	finish a supply of something
put weight on (11)	increase	work something out (8)	think about and plan
*put on an event/a show (9)	organize an event	work something out (12)	calculate
put a cigarette out (11)	extinguish		
put your hand up (11)	lift into the air		
put prices up (11)	increase		

Lexical phrase list

Come (Unit 7)

come as a big/a dreadful/
    a great/a nasty/a terrible shock
come as an enormous/a great/
    a welcome relief
come as no/a big/a great/a
    complete/a pleasant surprise
come in handy
come into fashion
come on
come to an agreement
come to a decision
come to an end
come to harm
come to nothing
come to power
come to the conclusion that
come to £20
come to terms with something
come true

Do (Unit 13)

do a course
do a deal
do a degree
do a job
do an exercise
do business with someone
do damage
do nothing
do some research
do someone a favour
do the cooking
do the housework
do the ironing
do the shopping
do the washing
do the washing up
do your best
do your homework

Get (Unit 1)

get angry/upset/bored/
    excited etc
get a cold/headache/
    the flu etc

get a job
get a (good/bad) mark in an
    exam/for a piece of work
get back
get (back) home
get better/worse/older etc
get dressed
get engaged/married/divorced
get going
get help
get in touch with someone
get in/out of a car/taxi
get into trouble (with the
    police)
get into/out of the habit of
    doing something
get on/off a bus/train/plane
get out of the habit of doing
    something
get paid
get ready (for work/school/
    Christmas)
get rid of something/someone
get someone down
get something for Christmas/
    your birthday
get something from a shop
get someone to help you
get started
get the bus/train/plane
get the chance to do
    something
get the dinner ready
get time to do something
get to school/work/a place
get to sleep

Give (Unit 9)

give a broad smile
give a deep sigh
give a lengthy speech
give a nervous laugh
give a party
give a piercing scream
give an example
give an impressive
    performance
give an open-air concert

give someone a blank look
give someone a call
give someone a hand
give someone an idea
give someone an injection (12)
give someone a lift
give someone a nasty shock
give someone a pleasant
    surprise
give someone a tender kiss
give someone expert advice
give someone full details
give someone great pleasure
give someone my best
    regards
give someone permission to
    do something
give someone a prescription (12)
give someone the impression that

Have (Unit 6)

have a dance (a bop)
have a go at doing something
have a good time
have a headache/sore throat
have a laugh
have a look
have a relationship
have a serious/a negative/an
    effect on someone/something
have a strong/important/good
    influence on someone/something
have a wash
have an insight into something
have an operation on part of your
    body
have difficulty (in) doing something
have fun
have one's arm/leg in plaster (12)
have problems doing something
have something in common
have sympathy for someone
have the power/energy/strength/
    authority to do something
have (no) time to do something
have a tooth taken out/filled
have something repaired

have your ear/nose pierced

have your hair cut/done/dyed

have your head shaved

have your house broken into

have your photo taken

have your tonsils taken out

It's got/it has nothing to do
    with you.

Can I have it back please?

What has she got on? (= What
    is she wearing?)

Make (Unit 13)

make a cake

make a complaint

make a cup of tea

make a choice

make a decision

make a film

make a loss

make a mess

make a mistake

make a noise

make a phone call

make a plan

make a profit

make a promise

make a speech

make a will

make an appointment

make an arrangement

make an effort

make an investment

make friends with someone

make fun of someone

make money

make some changes

make sure

make the beds

make up your mind

make yourself at home

Put (Unit 11)

can't/couldn't put my book
    down

put a lot of time/effort/hard work/
    energy into (doing) something

put a plaster on a cut (12)

put a record/CD/tape/video on

put one's feet up

put pressure on someone (to
    do something)

put some money to one side (13)

put someone's arm in plaster (12)

put someone/someone's health/
    life at risk

put someone in a good mood

put someone in touch with
    someone else

put someone on a course of
    antibiotics (12)

put someone up for the night

put the blame on someone for
    (doing) something

Take (Unit 4)

take a joke

take a long time to do
    something

take a photo

take a risk

take care of

take courage

take criticism

take interest in

take it or leave it

take my word for it

take notice of

take offence at

take one thing at a time

take part in something (2)

take pity on

take place (2)

take pride in

take someone's advice

take something back
    to a shop

take some medicine/a pill (12)

take something seriously

take someone's temperature (12)

take someone to a restaurant/
    out for a meal

take someone to hospital

take someone to school

take the blame for

take the infinitive/gerund

take time off work

take your time

I can't take it any more.

she/he won't take no for an answer

Irregular verb list

Infinitive	Past simple	Past participle	Infinitive	Past simple	Past participle
arise	arose	arisen	have	had	had
awake	awoke	awoken	hear	heard	heard
be	was/were	been	hide	hid	hidden
bear	bore	borne	hit	hit	hit
beat	beat	beaten	hold	held	held
become	became	become	hurt	hurt	hurt
begin	began	begun	keep	kept	kept
bend	bent	bent	kneel	knelt	knelt
bet	bet	bet	know	knew	known
bind	bound	bound	lay	laid	laid
bite	bit	bitten	lead	led	led
blow	blew	blown	lean	leant/leaned	leant/leaned
break	broke	broken	learn	learnt/learned	learnt/learned
breed	bred	bred	leave	left	left
bring	brought	brought	lend	lent	lent
build	built	built	let	let	let
burn	burnt/burned	burnt/burned	lie	lay	lain
burst	burst	burst	light	lit	lit
buy	bought	bought	lose	lost	lost
catch	caught	caught	make	made	made
choose	chose	chosen	mean	meant	meant
come	came	come	meet	met	met
cost	cost	cost	pay	paid	paid
creep	crept	crept	put	put	put
cut	cut	cut	seek	sought	sought
deal	dealt	dealt	show	showed	shown
dig	dug	dug	shrink	shrank/shrunk	shrunk
do	did	done	slide	slid	slid
draw	drew	drawn	smell	smelt/smelled	smelt/smelled
dream	dreamt/dreamed	dreamt/dreamed	sow	sowed	sown
drink	drank	drunk	speed	sped	sped
drive	drove	driven	spill	spilt/spilled	spilt/spilled
eat	ate	eaten	spin	spun	spun
fall	fell	fallen	spit	spat	spat
feed	fed	fed	split	split	split
feel	felt	felt	spoil	spoilt/spoiled	spoilt/spoiled
fight	fought	fought	spread	spread	spread
find	found	found	spring	sprang	sprung
flee	fled	fled	sting	stung	stung
fly	flew	flown	stink	stank/stunk	stunk
forbid	forbade	forbidden	strike	struck	struck
forget	forgot	forgotten	swear	swore	sworn
forgive	forgave	forgiven	sweep	swept	swept
freeze	froze	frozen	swell	swelled	swollen/swelled
get	got	got/gotten (AE)	swing	swung	swung
give	gave	given	take	took	taken
go	went	gone	tread	trod	trodden
grind	ground	ground	weave	wove	woven
grow	grew	grown	weep	wept	wept
hang	hung	hung	wind	wound	wound

126

Answer key

Reading: Gapped text, page 2

1

Name of Star	Former possessions
Cher	white T-shirt, black shirt (also mentioned: top, dress)
Mel Gibson	denim shirt
Cary Grant	silver cigarette case
'Dr McCoy'	tunic

2 1 D 2 B 3 H 4 F
  5 A 6 C 7 E G not used

3 1 celebrities 2 pick up 3 bargain
  4 memorabilia 5 purchase 6 shrank
  7 delighted 8 fancy dress

4 1 up as 2 to pieces 3 my eye on
  4 my heart

Vocabulary, page 4

A Clothes

1 1 shabby 2 scarf 3 tracksuit
  4 waterproof 5 blouse 6 plain
  7 helmet 8 belt 9 bracelet
  10 blazer 11 slippers 12 baseball cap

2 Suggested answers

1 a baggy jumper 2 a pleated skirt
3 a checked waistcoat 4 a flowery dress
5 tight-fitting jeans 6 striped swimming trunks
7 spotted socks

B Get

1 1 by 2 over 3 back 4 away
  5 on 6 off 7 out of

2 1 touch 2 trouble 3 paid 4 rid
  5 ready 6 mark 7 worse 8 dressed

C Word combinations

1 fashion/film industry
2 model/news agency
3 political/birthday party
4 television/job interview
5 social/sporting event
6 film/world premiere
7 news/bedtime story

Language focus, page 6

A Adverbs of frequency

1 correct
2 I have never been wearing
3 Her clothes are often quite tight on me/ Often her clothes are quite tight on me
4 I sometimes see/Sometimes I see
5 correct

B Used to and would

1 b (only *used to*)
2 c (neither *used to* or *would*)
3 a (both *used to* and *would*)
4 b (only *used to*)
5 b (only *used to*)

Use of English, page 6

Transformations

1 don't/do not usually eat much
2 hardly ever stay
3 always used to be
4 keeps (on) phoning me
5 's/is rare for Anna to
6 looking forward to going
7 not used to getting

B Multiple-choice cloze

1 B **2** D **3** C **4** A
5 D **6** C **7** A **8** B
9 B **10** A **11** D **12** C

Writing, page 8

Letters and emails

1

	Formal	Informal
Complaining	7	4
Asking for information	1	10
Giving information	5	9
Apologizing	3	6
Giving advice	8	2

2

Formal	Informal
1 inform me	**10** let me know
8 We strongly advise you not to	**2** You really shouldn't
3 the delay in responding to you	**6** it's taken me so long to get back to you
7 Moreover	**4** And
5 estimate	**9** reckon

Informal letters

2 Paragraph 1 a Paragraph 2 c Paragraph 3 b

Reading: Gapped text, page 10

1 1 C 2 G 3 A 4 E 5 H
  6 B 7 F D is not used

2 1 head 2 eye 3 foot
  4 arm 5 mouth 6 face

Vocabulary, page 11

A Music

1 trumpet	2 flute	3 violin
4 tambourine	5 drum	6 saxophone
7 keyboard	8 accordion	

B Sport

1 **a** athlete   **b** basketball player
   c cyclist   **d** golfer
   e gymnast   **f** skier
   g snowboarder   **h** tennis player

2 **1** *motor racing circuit*   **2** football pitch
   3 athletics track   **4** ski slope
   5 swimming pool   **6** golf course
   7 tennis court   **8** ice-skating rink

3 **1** B   **2** D   **3** A   **4** C
   5 C   **6** D   **7** A   **8** B

Language focus, page 12

A Indirect ways of asking questions

1 telling me what you have been doing recently?
2 where I can get something cold to drink?
3 what time you are coming to the party next week?
4 to me why you did not do the homework?
5 if you are interested in playing tennis on Friday.
6 what he does for a living.

B Gerunds and infinitives

1 looking, to have
2 learning, to speak, to think
3 to be, climbing, attracting, to wait
4 making, to concentrate
5 going, to stay
6 Giving, to lose/losing
7 to hear, seeing
8 to paint, forgetting, to buy
9 to live, to find, to pay
10 to work, going

Use of English, page 13

Open cloze: Prepositions

1 in	2 on	3 for	4 into	5 in
6 in	7 on	8 on	9 at	10 out
11 in	12 in	13 at	14 with	15 until

Transformations

1 help laughing
2 to take up (playing) golf
3 'm/am not (very) keen on
4 can't stand being

5 's/is unusual for Andrea to
6 to take place
7 'm/am not very good at

Word formation

1 irrelevant	2 disagreement
3 misunderstood	4 dishonestly
5 unreliable	6 immature
7 overweight	8 undercooked
9 irresponsibly	10 incapable

Writing, page 15

A Formal and informal style

1 a	2 a	3 b	4 b	5 b
6 a	7 b	8 a	9 a	

B An informal letter

3 b, **8** a, **7** b, (new paragraph) **1** a, **6** a, **9** a, **2** a, (new paragraph) **4** b, (new paragraph) **5** b

Dear Nick

(3b) Thanks for sending me the advert about skiing in Nevis Range. (8a) It sounds just the sort of place I'm looking for. (7b) But before I book, there are a few things I'd like to ask you.

(1a) Firstly, as I'm not an experienced skier, I'd really like to know how many green runs there are. (6a) I wanted to ask you some questions about costs, as well. **I'm a bit broke at the moment, so the holiday needs to as cheap as possible.** (9a) Do you think I'd save much by getting the bus from London instead of the train? (2a) And can you remember if the skis cost a lot to hire? **If they're too expensive, I'll ask a friend to lend me hers.**

(4b) Finally, I'm only planning to go skiing for three days, so can you tell me if you think it's worth having classes. **I suppose it depends on the instructors – were they good?**

(5b) Thanks for all your help. Write back soon.

All the best

Caroline

C Building on the information given

1 between 6a and 9a
2 between 2a and 4b
3 between 4b and 5b

D Linking words and expressions

Informal	Formal
as well	in addition
and	in addition (to this)
as	owing to the fact that
so	therefore
but	however

Unit 3

Reading: Multiple matching, page 18

1 **a** A, B, D, F   **b** C, E

2 **1** A   **2** C   **3** B   **4** E
5/6 A, F in any order
7 D   **8** C   **9** A   **10** E   **11** B
12 A   **13/14/15** D, E, F in any order

3 **1** e   **2** a   **3** c   **4** d   **5** b

4 **1** get by   **2** came out   **3** take up
4 brought, up   **5** took over

Vocabulary, page 20

Technology

Across	Down
1 handy	**1** headphones
3 DVD	**2** dial
7 laptop	**4** disposable
9 out	**5** remote
10 surf	**6** IT
11 on	**8** portable
12 log	**10** system
13 satellite	

Language focus, page 20

A Articles

1 The, a, –, the
2 –, –, –, a, a, The, a, the, –, the
3 –, the, a
4 a, a, the, The, a
5 the, –, a, an

B Comparisons

1 hard   **2** hottest   **3** more careful
4 better   **5** soon   **6** most boring
7 more tired/tireder   **8** earlier
9 fastest   **10** quieter/more quiet

C Comparative expressions

1 b   **2** d   **3** e   **4** a   **5** c

D Correcting mistakes

1 Walkman
This invention <u>which</u> completely changed
But <u>however</u> its creator
the portable device, <u>more</u> smaller than

2 Compass
This device was the most <u>of</u> important
to <u>can</u> know
the most significant <u>of</u> event

3 Video
significantly <u>very</u> cheaper
nearly as <u>most</u> common
as <u>more</u> often as they like

4 Space blanket
a type of <u>the</u> plastic
It is used <u>to</u>, for example
as a result of <u>the</u> Man's efforts

5 Radar
and is used <u>for</u> to detect
as an instrument <u>as</u> of war
In addition <u>to</u>,

Use of English, page 22

Transformations

1 not nearly as/so difficult
2 not as many girls
3 least comfortable chair in
4 I smoke, the more
5 lives further/farther (away) from
6 did much worse than
7 not earn as much as
8 the cleverest person I have/I've

Open cloze

1 b

2 **1** used   **2** it   **3** The   **4** well
5 be   **6** on   **7** later   **8** from
9 The/These/Such   **10** an
11 that/which   **12** as

Word formation

1 skilful/skilled   **2** technological
3 tasty   **4** helpless
5 inventor   **6** later
7 appearance   **8** electrician
9 successful   **10** widely

Writing, page 24

2 Essay: **1** e   **2** g   **3** b   **4** d
Article: **1** f   **2** a   **3** h   **4** c

3 Essay
Formal linkers (However, On the one hand/On
the other hand, In addition, Moreover)
Article
Phrasal verbs (couldn't do without, get by)
Informal linkers (And, But, So)
Direct questions (Can you imagine an object in
your house which you dislike having to use but
which you know you couldn't do without?)

Unit 4

Reading: Multiple choice, page 26

1
1 B	**2** D	**3** C	**4** D
5 A	**6** C	**7** C	**8** B

2
a unequivical
b seminal
c dismissive
d chilling
e clumsy
f literate
g trendy
h lofty

Vocabulary, page 28

A Cinema and films

1 cast	**2** plot	**3** make-up
4 scene	**5** comedy	**6** effects
7 part	**8** stuntman	**9** office
10 remake	**11** soundtrack	

B Expressions with *take*

1
1 interest	**2** offence	**3** pity
4 blame	**5** care	**6** notice
7 advice	**8** joke	**9** courage
10 risk		

C Phrasal verbs with *take*

1 after	**2** up	**3** to
4 over	**5** on	**6** up

Language focus, page 29

A Tenses

1
1 had been living, started, was training, met
2 heard, phoned, had got, told, had taken
3 were watching, went, had forgotten
4 got, had eaten, had already left, were still dancing

2
1 told	**2** had passed
3 took	**4** were waiting
5 went	**6** had finished
7 started	**8** was holding
9 had got	**10** had, driven
11 was sitting	**12** was

B *So* and *such*

1 so much homework
2 so few people
3 such delicious food (that)
4 such a good
5 so interested in the book

C Linking words

1 for	**2** As
3 In the end	**4** at last
5 After	**6** afterwards

Use of English, page 30

Word formation

1 frightening	**2** embarrassed
3 increasingly	**4** tiring, exhausted
5 uninteresting	**6** surprisingly
7 confused	**8** annoying, unconvincing, impressed

Multiple-choice cloze

1 C	**2** A	**3** C	**4** B
5 B	**6** C	**7** D	**8** B
9 C	**10** A	**11** D	**12** B

Writing, page 32

1b Advantages of book:
Can read anywhere and at anytime/more entertainment from a book – lasts long time
Advantages of a film version:
Visual – makes story more memorable
Special effects – all scenes in book are possible
Disadvantages of film:
Film not always good interpretation
Film cuts and changes to story
Disadvantages of book:
Too much effort needed

2b
1 Many people prefer going to **the** cinema
2 **On** the one hand,
3 books help **(to) develop** your imagination
4 You can decide what ~~do~~ the characters
5 the characters and places in the story **look** like
6 the enjoyment from a book lasts ~~more~~ longer
7 they **sometimes** cut
8 the most **interesting** parts
9 special effects are **so** good
10 ~~the~~ most scenes of a book
11 a book can ~~to~~ be shown
12 less effort **than** reading
13 it is **always** better
14 **Afterwards/After that** you can see it
15 if you want **to** compare

Unit 5

Reading: multiple matching, page 34

1 **1** E   **2** B   **3** A   **4** D   **5** F   **6** C/E
    7 C/E   **8** B   **9** E   **10** A   **11** C/D   **12** C/D
    13 E   **14** C/F   **15** C/F

2 **1** player
    2 computer
    3 simulator
    4 supervisor
    5 manager
    6 instructor

3 **1** scanner   **6** demonstrator
    2 calculator   **7** competitor
    3 adviser/advisor **8** photocopier
    4 inventor   **9** researcher
    5 presenter   **10** spectator

Vocabulary, page 36

A Jobs crossword

Across		Down	
1	dustman	**2**	teacher
6	baker	**3**	waitress
8	hairdresser	**4**	lawyer
9	chef	**5**	butcher
11	accountant	**7**	surgeon
		10	vet

B Questions and answers

1 **1** e   **2** g   **3** a   **4** c
    5 f   **6** h   **7** b   **8** d

2 judge, politician, company director
    (other answers may be acceptable)

C Expressions with *work*

1 worked, overtime
2 worked for myself
3 to work long hours
4 working part-time, working full-time
5 to work flexitime
6 works shifts
7 working my way up

Language focus, page 37

Obligation, necessity and permission

1 **1** should/need to
    2 have to/need to
    3 need to
    4 must
    5 Do we have to/Should we
    6 had to
    7 must, to have to
    8 must/should

2 **1** *can, must*
    2 shouldn't, must
    3 can, can't
    4 needn't, must
    5 can, should
    6 can't, must

Use of English, page 38

Transformations

1 are not/aren't allowed to smoke
2 are they supposed to
3 had/'d better not drink
4 ought to have/show more
5 won't/don't let me stay
6 used to make me tidy
7 was made to clean

Word formation

1 assistant		**2** exciting
3 advertisement		**4** patience
5 ability		**6** annoyed
7 carefully		**8** being
9 confidence		**10** learner
11 Unfortunately		**12** intolerant
13 angry		**14** satisfying

Open cloze

1 as	**2** a	**3** made	**4** had
5 our	**6** take	**7** up	**8** us
9 get	**10** at	**11** there	**12** as

Writing, page 40

1 **a** No – apart from *A woman was speaking* and *they wouldn't know*, everything is in the past simple.

   b No – basic vocabulary and some words (*couldn't, nice, phone, speak*) are repeated.

   c No – only *and* (6 times), *then* and *but*. Most sentences are very short.

   d No – the story is written as only one paragraph.

2

I was beginning to feel a little nervous. It was my first day **(1)** <u>as the personal assistant to a company director</u>. I **(2)** <u>had claimed</u> at <u>the interview</u> that I could speak French but **(3)** <u>it wasn't true</u>. I hoped they wouldn't **(4)** <u>find out</u> that I **(5)** <u>had been lying</u>.

At first everything went well. My boss was very **(6)** <u>helpful</u> and he **(7)** <u>explained to</u> me what I had to do. **Then** he introduced me to **(8)** <u>my colleagues</u>, **who** were all very **(9)** <u>friendly</u>. **Just as** I was sitting down at my desk the phone rang.

As soon as I (10) picked up the receiver I started to panic. A woman was speaking to me in French and **naturally**, I couldn't understand (11) a word she was saying. **When** the boss saw (12) how upset I was, he took the phone from me.

To my surprise he (13) answered the woman in English and then he (14) burst out laughing. **Afterwards** he told me it was his mother. She (15) had just been to the dentist's and (16) was having difficulty speaking properly. She (17) had been talking to me in English not French!

3 The answer to all four questions, **a–d**, is now Yes.

Unit 6

Reading: Gapped text, page 42

1 **1** G   **2** B   **3** F   **4** A
       5 E   **6** H   **7** C   D not used

2 Words for male relatives: *nephew*, uncle, son, father/Dad, brothers, husband, grandfather

Words for female relatives: *sister-in-law*, aunt, daughter, Mum, sisters, wife, nieces

Words for both male and female relatives: *grandparent*, cousin/second cousin, children, parents, (nearest and dearest)

3 **1** close   Different **a** /kləʊs/, **b** /kləʊz/
       2 too   Same
       3 live   Different **a** /lɪv/, **b** /laɪv/
       4 mean   Same
       5 matches Same
       6 used   Different **a** /juːst/, **b** /juːzd/
       7 book   Same
       8 fair   Same

Vocabulary, page 44

A Adjectives of personality

1 fussy   **2** bossy   **3** clumsy
4 stubborn   **5** dull   **6** reserved
7 ambitious   **8** affectionate

B Compound adjectives

1 broad-shouldered   **2** left-handed
3 fair-haired   **4** round-faced
5 heart-shaped   **6** brown-eyed
7 shoulder-length   **8** well-known

C Expressions with *have*

1 an operation   **2** a look
3 the strength   **4** difficulty
5 influence   **6** a go
7 common   **8** sympathy

Language focus, page 45

A Causative *have*

1 We had our car repaired yesterday.
2 I want to have my photo taken.
3 She has (*or* had) never had her ears pierced before.
4 I'm having (*or* I'm going to have) my hair cut at 5 o'clock tomorrow.
5 They'll probably have (*or* They're probably going to have) their house painted next month.
6 I always have my suits made in Milan now.

B Phrasal verbs

1 a I'm very fond of my grandmother. I've always **looked up to her**.
2 a I think I **take after my father** rather than my mother.
3 b I don't earn a great deal but **I get by**.
4 a I blame the parents. They haven't **brought him up** very well.
5 b He looked so lovely in the pet shop; I **fell for him** immediately.
6 b These meetings **take up** too much time.

C Relative clauses

1 who, which   **2** who/that, whose
3 where, which/that   **4** why, when
5 which, where   **6** who/that, which/that
7 which/that, which, whose

Commas are required in the following sentences:

1 after *Mr Jones* and *15 years*
4 after *January*
5 after *The fox* and *shy animal* and *residential areas*
7 after *on Friday* and *my eldest sister*

Use of English, page 47

Multiple-choice cloze

1 B   **2** D   **3** D   **4** B   **5** C   **6** D
7 A   **8** C   **9** D   **10** A   **11** B   **12** B

Transformations

1 not tall enough to be
2 there was too much
3 had our house broken into
4 to have my hair dyed
5 for whom I have
6 whose cat I rescued
7 look up to
8 let them down

Writing, page 48

2 **1** g   **2** b, f, a, d   **3** h, j   **4** c, i   **5** e
3 **a** sincerely   **b** faithfully

Unit 7

Reading: Multiple matching, page 50

1 **1** B **2** D **3** A **4** C
  5/6 A, D in any order **7** B
  8/9 A, C in any order **10** B
  11 A **12/13** C, D in any order
  14/15 C, D in any order

2 **1** d **2** f **3** e **4** b **5** a **6** c

3 **1** turned into **2** put up with
  3 moved out **4** springing up
  5 cut down, cut out

4 **1** I've had words with them
  2 came to an agreement
  3 I've got my eye on
  4 put (our flat) up for sale
  5 I'm on first-name terms with
  6 it's getting beyond a joke

Vocabulary, page 51

A Wordsearch

T	T	T	S	I	R	O	L	F	G
F	R	T	I	I	E	A	E	R	C
R	O	N	G	L	L	A	O	G	H
E	L	E	O	F	L	C	E	R	E
T	L	G	O	I	E	H	L	E	C
N	E	A	D	R	W	E	S	H	K
U	Y	S	S	E	C	I	C	O
O	H	W	A	H	J	K	A	T	U
C	H	E	M	I	S	T	A	U	T
C	N	N	I	A	G	R	A	B	T

Shopkeepers:
baker, butcher, chemist, florist, grocer, jeweller, news-agent

Things in shops or supermarkets:
aisle, bargain, checkout, counter, goods, till, trolley

B Multiple choice

1 B **2** C **3** C **4** A **5** B **6** D
7 A **8** D **9** B **10** A

C Phrasal verbs with *come*

1 down **2** across **3** up **4** up **5** round

D Expressions with *come*

1 come in handy **2** come on
3 come into fashion **4** come to terms with
5 come true **6** come to

E Word formation: Nouns

	Verb	Noun
1	try	trial
2	cure	cure
3	like	liking
4	split	split
5	consult	consultant
6	announce	announcement
7	behave	behaviour
8	create	creation
9	assist	assistant
10	appear	appearance

  a liking **b** announcement **c** trial
  d behaviour **e** creation

Language focus, page 53

A Contrasting ideas

1 B **2** B and C **3** A
4 C **5** A and B **6** A and C

B The present perfect and past simple

1 has just published **2** has changed
3 has increased **4** (were) expected
5 lived **6** has risen
7 has doubled **8** have been
9 disappeared **10** has become
11 was **12** has taken
13 had **14** were
15 stood

C Correcting mistakes

1 My father's been working/has worked
2 I've broken my leg
3 Charlie Chaplin was one of the greatest
4 how long I've been waiting
5 the first time I have seen this film
6 known each other for many years
7 since I last played football
8 I have cleaned three rooms

Use of English, page 55

Transformations

1 come to a decision
2 although he is unable
3 despite the train being
4 to walk rather than catch
5 not leave yet
6 has been learning French for
7 last time we saw
8 since I (last) had

Word formation

1 picturesque **2** inhabitants
3 beautiful **4** neighbourhood
5 peaceful **6** pleasant

7 disadvantages	8 infrequent
9 dependent	10 unfriendly

Open cloze

1 a	2 to	3 than
4 a/each/every/per	5 are	6 more
7 for	8 how	9 what
10 If/Should	11 not	12 which

Writing, page 56

A Structure

Paragraph **1** d	Paragraph **2** a
Paragraph **3** c	Paragraph **4** b

B Language analysis

a adjectives: *competitive*, fast, efficient, useful, informative, handy

modifiers: *extremely (competitive)*, particularly (useful), very (informative), fairly (good), especially (handy)

adverbs of frequency: *normally*, always, sometimes, usually, often

b **1** about **2** fact **3** Personally **4** anyone

Unit 8

Reading: Multiple choice, page 58

1

1 C **2** A **3** C **4** D **5** B **6** B **7** D **8** A

2

a took up

b catch up on

c put off

d used up

e picked up

Vocabulary, page 60

Confusing words

1 fun	2 crowded	3 campsite	4 holiday
5 stay	6 resort	7 souvenirs	8 views
9 trip	10 cruise		

Language focus, page 60

The future

1

1 I'll put

2 you're going to have

3 We're meeting/We're going to meet

4 you leave

5 I'll get/I'm going to get

6 we'll be sitting

7 are you doing/are you going to do

8 I'll have spoken

2

1 'll/will carry

2 'm/am having

3 ends, 'll be

4 'll be watching, will/'ll have finished

5 'm going to get

6 gets

7 will/'ll have been travelling, 'll/will want

8 'll be/'m going to be

Use of English, page 61

Transformations

1 am/'m (really) looking forward to

2 are/'re likely to take him

3 by bus makes up

4 to set up

5 if they get on

6 come up with

7 to give up smoking

8 split up with

Open cloze

1 in	2 a/each/every/per
3 off	4 well
5 than	6 with
7 not	8 is
9 as	10 which
11 whose	12 one

Word formation

1 loosened	2 lengthen	3 worsened
4 sharpening	5 depths	6 thickens
7 deafness	8 reddened	9 brightened
10 tightening		

Writing, page 63

A Model

a congratulate you on **b** with regard to

c you could also perhaps mention

d it is true **e** it is worth

f you claim that **g** no longer the case

B Analysis

1 However, but, although

2 Firstly, In addition, Finally

3 a with regard to

b it is true that

c no longer the case

C Adding relevant information

the gifts: *the handmade knives for which the area is famous*

the restaurant: *the portions are usually very large*

the river: *It has recently been cleaned and in some places it is possible to swim.*

Unit 9

Reading: Multiple matching, page 66

1   **1** D   **2** H   **3** B   **4** F
    5 A   **6** G   **7** C   E not used

2
a struck (infinitive: strike)   **b** tricking
c account for   **d** glow   **e** cited
f log   **g** flows   **h** hover

3
1 tricked   **2** cited   **3** hovering
4 struck   **5** accounted for   **6** flows
7 glow/glowing   **8** log

Vocabulary, page 68

A Phrasal verbs

1 c   **2** e   **3** a   **4** g   **5** b   **6** d   **7** f

B Expressions with *give*

1 example   **2** lift
3 hand   **4** permission
5 impression   **6** call
7 idea

C Collocations

1 blank   **2** broad
3 nervous   **4** piercing
5 deep   **6** full
7 impressive

D Revision: *Get*

1 down   **2** over   **3** away   **4** by

Language focus, page 69

A Modal verbs of speculation

1
1 might have left
2 correct
3 could/may/might have gone away
4 correct
5 correct
6 may/might not be the right size
7 can't/couldn't be going out with Sue
8 correct
9 He must have decided
10 correct

2 Possible answers
1 He can't have slept very well.
   He must have been working very hard.
   He might have been driving all day.
2 She could be on a diet.
   She may have split up with her boyfriend.
   She might not be feeling very well.

3 The bus and train drivers might be on strike.
   Everyone must have decided to drive to work today.
   There may be a special event taking place.
4 It must be too hot for them.
   You can't have watered them enough.
   They might have some kind of disease.
5 Their son must have got into trouble again.
   They might have caught the burglar that broke into their house.
   They may have been looking for someone.
6 He might have found a job.
   He must be going out with someone.
   He could have won the lottery.
7 They might be drunk.
   They may be having an argument.
   Someone might have been robbed.
8 You must have parked it somewhere else.
   Someone may have stolen it.
   The police might have taken it away.

B Question tags

1 has he   **2** aren't I
3 doesn't he   **4** wouldn't you
5 didn't she   **6** will you
7 will/would/can you   **8** shall we
9 did it   **10** do they

Use of English, page 70

Multiple-choice cloze

1 A   **2** C   **3** A   **4** D
5 C   **6** B   **7** A   **8** C
9 D   **10** B   **11** B   **12** A

Word formation

1
1 humorous   humorously
2 ambitious   ambitiously
3 beneficial   beneficially
4 hungry   hungrily
5 anxious   anxiously
6 original   originally

2

	Verb	Noun	Adjective +	Adjective −
1	attract	attraction	attractive	unattractive
2	decide	decision	decisive	indecisive
3	excite	excitement	exciting/ed	unexciting/ed
4	imagine	imagination	imaginative	unimaginative
5	obey	obedience	obedient	disobedient
6	offend	offence	offensive	inoffensive
7	please	pleasure	pleasant	unpleasant
8	succeed	success	successful	unsuccessful
9	think	thought	thoughtful	thoughtless
10	tolerate	tolerance	tolerant	intolerant

3

1 unattractive	**2** decisions
3 excitement	**4** imaginatively
5 disobedient	**6** offence
7 pleasures	**8** successfully
9 thoughtful	**10** intolerant

Writing, page 72

A Model

1 opinion	**2** think	**3** However
4 argument	**5** extent	**6** hand
7 Moreover	**8** although	**9** conclude

The words used to introduce the three examples are:
such as Carnival, like the 'Fallas',
For example, Bonfire Night

B Organization

The writer follows plan B.

C Ideas

A 1, 5, 7, 11 all agree
B 2, 4, 9, 12 all disagree
C 3, 6, 8, 10 all disagree

Unit 10

Reading: Multiple matching, page 74

1

1 E	**2** C	**3/4** A, E in any order	**5** D
6 E	**7** D	**8** B	**9** C	**10/11** A, B in any order
12 D	**13** E	**14** A	**15** D

2

1 a	**2** c	**3** e	**4** b	**5** f	**6** d

3

1 snatched	**2** squirt	**3** waving	**4** Unaware
5 stuck	**6** pointed		

4

get in touch with someone/get lucky/get back (to the hotel)/get out
hold one's nose/hold tightly onto the camera
pick the wrong person/pick something up
take off a jacket/take someone to a place/take a wallet
make a mess/make the mistake of doing something
have fun/have no idea (what someone is on about)

5

1 in touch	**2** tightly on to	**3** them up
4 me to	**5** the mistake	**6** no idea

Vocabulary, page 76

A Crime

1 pickpocketing	**2** arson
3 robbery	**4** burglary
5 kidnap	**6** blackmail
7 smuggling	**8** drug trafficking

B Phrasal verbs

1

1 take in	**2** look into
3 get away with	**4** make out
5 make up	**6** take up
7 look up to	**8** get up to

2

1 making (it) up	**2** make out	**3** taken in
4 get away with	**5** looking into	**6** getting up to

Language focus, page 77

A Active and passive

1 was released, being found, did not commit/had not committed
2 is being repaired, was told, won't/wouldn't be
3 have been asked, haven't prepared
4 happened, were caught, were made, took
5 are produced, are sold, are exported
6 was given, died, stopped, hasn't been fixed
7 is thought, was found, was walking
8 destroyed, didn't do/haven't done, be allowed

B Revision: Modal verbs

1 needn't have revised
2 didn't need to pay
3 don't have to go
4 mustn't tell
5 shouldn't have
6 needn't have bought
7 needn't worry/don't need to worry
8 didn't have to go

Use of English, page 78

Transformations

1 was not/wasn't given
2 is/'s being met
3 was robbed (by thieves) of
4 is being looked into
5 had been made up by
6 is said to be
7 are expected to be announced
8 is believed to have
9 is thought to have known
10 needn't have taken
11 we didn't need to

Word formation

1 buildings	**2** residential	**3** amazing
4 reduction	**5** robbery	**6** effective
7 criminals	**8** presence	**9** invasion
10 evidence		

Open cloze

1 who/that	**2** has	**3** not/never	**4** being
5 such	**6** or	**7** the/its	**8** is
9 take	**10** for	**11** are	**12** made

Writing, page 80

Student B's answer would be given a higher mark.

A Analysis

	A	B
1	no	yes
2	yes	yes
3	no	yes
4	no	yes
5	no	yes
6	no	yes
7	no	yes
8	yes	yes
9	no	yes
10	no	yes

B Accuracy

a I **arrived** at the station
  to catch the train
  I **was feeling/felt** sad
  I **had finished** my holiday
  I **decided** to go
  make me **feel**
  somebody **had stolen** it
  I **felt** sadder

b **at** the station
  because I had finished
  I enjoyed the holiday
  want to come home
  the shop to buy
  suitcase **on** the ground
  paid the woman
  to finish **a** holiday

C Addressing the reader

Did you get my postcard from Italy?
You'll never guess what happened to me after I'd posted it to you!
… you know how unfit I am!
You can imagine how relieved I felt.
How about you, Esther? Did anything exciting happen on your holiday? Write and tell me all about it.

Unit 11

Reading: Gapped text, page 82

1 H	**2** E	**3** A	**4** G
5 F	**6** D	**7** B	C not used

2

1 developments	**2** survival
3 participants	**4** passionately
5 global	**6** anywhere
7 awareness	**8** technological

3

Verb	Noun
entertain	entertainment
refuse	refusal
assist	assistant
occupy	occupant
enjoy	enjoyment
replace	replacement
approve	approval
deny	denial
arrange	arrangement
inhabit	inhabitant

4

1 inhabitants	**2** approval	**3** enjoyment
4 denial	**5** occupants	

Vocabulary, page 84

A Crossword: The weather

Across	Down
1 drought	**2** hail
6 flood	**3** clouds
7 gale	**4** tidal
8 severe	**5** breeze
9 choppy	**6** forecast
11 fine	**10** pour
12 struck	
13 gust	

B The environment

1

1 c	**2** d	**3** f	**4** a
5 b	**6** e		

2

1 e	**2** d	**3** a	**4** f
5 b	**6** h	**7** g	**8** c

3

1 exhaust fumes
2 oil slick
3 dog mess
4 greenhouse effect
5 power station
6 nature reserve

Language focus, page 85

A So, neither and nor

1

1 c	2 e	3 d	4 h
5 g	6 a	7 b	8 f

2

1 *neither can I*	2 so is
3 neither/nor does	4 so are
5 so did	6 neither/nor will
7 so has	8 neither/nor would
9 so had	

B Conditionals

1

1 *had, would help*
2 will buy, promise
3 hadn't said, wouldn't have got
4 sleeps, is usually
5 had gone, would have met
6 beat, will go
7 press, underlines/will underline
8 were, would go
9 will be, get
10 hadn't taken, would have got

2 Suggested answers

2 We would have gone sailing if there had been enough wind.
3 If I wasn't afraid of flying, we would go abroad on holiday.
4 If he hadn't broken his leg, he could drive.
5 I could have taken some photos if I had remembered to pack my camera.
6 If he had a suit, he would go to the wedding.
7 He wouldn't be feeling ill if he hadn't drunk so much last night.
8 She could have gone to university if she'd passed her exams.
9 If they'd watched the news, they would have heard about the earthquake.

3 Possible answers

1 I would probably miss my family.
2 I would try to improve the health system.
3 I hadn't come to this school.
4 they gave us an extra week's holiday in summer.
5 I'll spend it on computer games.
6 I wouldn't be able to send emails to my friends in Australia.

Use of English, page 87

Multiple-choice cloze

1 B	2 D	3 C	4 D

5 B	6 C	7 B	8 A
9 C	10 D	11 D	12 A

Transformations

1 so did
2 put me up
3 put the concert off/put off the concert
4 more time into
5 's/has been raining heavily
6 won't/will not go swimming unless
7 had enough money
8 his brother hadn't/had not told

Writing, page 88

2 Features

- A relevant title:
  The highs and lows of mountain weather
- Questions to involve the reader:
  … what would be your favourite type of weather?
  Glorious sunshine to sunbathe in?
  Deep snow to ski in?
  And what would you find it hard to put up with?
  Who wouldn't feel bad-tempered by the end of it all?
- A range of vocabulary related to the weather:
  glorious sunshine, deep snow, fine or heavy, spitting or pouring, wet weather, the sun comes out, a shower, wind … blows
- Elements of informal language:
  it's, there's, wouldn't, I'd
  And, But, put up with
- Examples to illustrate a point:
  Clothes are blown off washing lines, etc
- Adverbs expressing opinion or attitude:
  Surprisingly

4

Extract a   Writing competition (page 88)
Consistent. An informal style.

Extract b   People and places (page 89)
Inconsistent. Begins with a more formal style, but ends informally.

Extract c   Competition (page 89)
Consistent. A neutral narrative style.

Unit 12

Reading: Multiple choice, page 90

1

1 C	2 B	3 D	4 B
5 A	6 C	7 C	8 A

2

1 against	2 in, of	3 of	4 on
5 for	6 with	7 on	8 for

Vocabulary, page 91

A Food

1 *bitter*	2 greasy	3 rich	
4 savoury	5 sour	6 sickly	
7 crunchy	8 spicy	9 stodgy	10 bland

B Health

1 damaged	2 hurting	3 aches
4 wounding	5 injuries	6 pains

C Have, put, give and take

1 e	2 d	3 g	4 a	5 b
6 h	7 f	8 c		

D Word formation: nouns

1 involvement	2 disappearance
3 obligation	4 seriousness
5 comparison	6 popularity
7 permission	8 retirement

Language focus, page 93

A Countable and uncountable nouns

1	a	2	a large number
3	Every	4	suggestion, accommodation
5	bar	6	few, much
7	no, a few	8	little
9	any more	10	another

B Reported speech

1

1 why did you apply/why have you applied for this job?
2 I'm thinking of going
3 I want to have
4 do you have/have you got
5 was (very) useful
6 helped me to understand what it's like
7 What are your main strengths?
8 have a lot of patience
9 I'm a very reliable

2

1 they did to keep fit
2 he was competing in a marathon the next/following day
3 (that) she did aerobics
4 she was thinking of taking up jogging
5 if/whether they could give us
6 eating/that we should eat/us to eat
7 her students not to eat
8 if they thought diets were
9 he had never needed to go on one
10 she had been on a diet once
11 she would not do it again
12 liked eating

Use of English, page 95

Open cloze

1 few	2 From	3 order
4 course	5 do	6 which
7 being	8 it	9 much
10 to	11 one	12 be

Transformations

1 had to wear
2 they had been trying
3 where she had bought her
4 warned him not to
5 (that) I (should) lie down
6 not give me very much

Writing, page 96

A Planning

1

1 B	2 A	3 C

B Writing

1 b	2 c	3 a

Unit 13

Reading: Multiple matching, page 98

1

1/2 C, E in any order	3 A
4/5 B, E in any order	6/7 A, D in any order
8 F	9 C
10/11 A, F in any order	12/13 D, E in any order
14/15 B, E in any order	

2

1 to put some money to one side
2 Money's a bit tight
3 to make ends meet
4 looking a million dollars
5 hard-up
6 came into
7 have money to burn
8 the jackpot
9 we're made of money
10 money grows on trees

Vocabulary, page 99

A Money

1

1 change	2 debt	3 bill	4 on loan
5 owe	6 coin	7 do	8 sell

2

1 *the receipt*   **2** coin   **3** owe   **4** on loan
5 bill   **6** change   **7** debt

B Revision: Lexical phrases

1 *taken, given*   **2** made, came
3 took, had   **4** having, getting, do
5 doing, put   **6** come, putting, get
7 gave, made

Language focus, page 100

A Ability

1 correct
2 Trevor was able to/managed to mend/succeeded in mending
3 correct
4 correct
5 correct
6 I've never been able to swim
7 he's incapable of organizing
8 correct
9 she won't be able to come/she can't come
10 They didn't succeed in getting

B Phrasal verbs and prepositions

1 off	**2** round	**3** for	**4** up
5 up	**6** for	**7** for	**8** out
9 of	**10** on	**11** for	**12** from
13 for	**14** from	**15** on	

Use of English, page 102

Multiple-choice cloze

1 B	**2** D	**3** B	**4** A
5 A	**6** D	**7** B	**8** D
9 C	**10** A	**11** B	**12** A

Word formation

1 highest	**2** amazed	**3** surprisingly
4 injuries	**5** broken	**6** survival
7 disbelief	**8** death	**9** reasonably
10 relief		

Transformations

1 made up our minds
2 made several telephone calls
3 was a difficult choice
4 no proof of
5 congratulated the players on winning
6 me for forgetting her birthday
7 didn't/did not succeed in reaching
8 's/is capable of running

Writing, page 104

2 **4** Introduction (or Aim)
   3 Sightseeing
   1 Shopping
   5 Lunch
   2 Conclusion

Different ways of referring to the tourists:
those who would rather go shopping, senior citizens, the visitors, the group, everyone, a group of elderly tourists, non-vegetarians

Different ways of making recommendations:
it is to be recommended, visitors can enjoy …
Non-vegetarians should try …

Words expressing number or quantity:
wide range of goods, a number of exclusive gift shops, numerous exhibits, one of several restaurants, one of the many fresh fish dishes

Words and expressions related to cost:
exclusive gift shops, generous discounts, reasonably priced lunch

3 b Target reader: the teacher in charge
   Style: formal
   Differences:

1	**3 a**
elderly tourists	young foreign students
for the morning	for the afternoon and evening
sightseeing	entertainment
	little money to spend

3 c Words to describe prices:
   reasonable, affordable, competitive

   Words to describe goods:
   cut-price, inexpensive

   Other words and expressions:
   good bargains, discounts, special offers
   good value for money

Unit 14

Reading: Gapped text, page 106

1   **1** C   **2** G   **3** E   **4** A   **5** F
   6 H   **7** D   B not used

2

1 set up	**2** take over
3 cut off	**4** get over
5 look after	**6** come up with

3

Adjective	Noun	Verb	Noun
cruel	cruelty	treat	treatment
pregnant	pregnancy	adopt	adoption
intelligent	intelligence	survive	survival
healthy	health	inspire	inspiration

Vocabulary, page 108

A Crossword: The Arts

Across	Down
1 sculptor	**1** stage
4 play	**2** priceless
6 scene	**3** orchestra
7 house	**4** portrait
8 landscape	**5** composer
10 exhibition	**7** hall
	9 cast

B Phrasal verbs: Revision

1 **a** take up **b** put off **c** do up
d make out **e** get on with **f** make up
g put up

2 **1** do up **2** get on with **3** taking up
4 made out **5** put off **6** make up
7 putting up **8** fall for

Language focus, page 109

1

1 had **2** wouldn't make
3 had brought **4** knew
5 would stop **6** didn't tell
7 go **8** bought

2 Suggested answers
1 *started revising for my exams.*
2 bought a watch.
3 came round after the film has finished.
4 would stop interrupting me.
5 the FCE exam were on a different day.
6 I'd insured the video camera.
7 the bus would hurry up and come/I'd caught the train.
8 I'd got someone to water the plants.

Use of English, page 110

Word formation

1 sculptures **2** best
3 considerable **4** decision
5 possibly **6** daily
7 residents **8** sight
9 irresponsible **10** beneficial

Open cloze

1 some **2** their **3** many
4 it **5** for **6** be
7 as **8** which **9** No
10 Although **11** there **12** in

Transformations

1 generosity impressed us very
2 a full recovery
3 had no choice (about) where
4 despite the late arrival/the lateness of
5 he had/has no intention of
6 of/about the exact depth

Writing, page 111

Language preparation

a **1** aim of this report
2 looking forward to
3 have no experience of
4 that struck me
5 pleased to hear
6 sum up
7 I like most about her
8 express an interest
9 obvious choice
10 main difference

b **1** 3 **2** 1 **3** 2 **4** 4 **5** 1
6 3 **7** 4 **8** 2 **9** 5b **10** 5a

Unit 15

Reading: Multiple choice, page 114

1 **1** C **2** A **3** D **4** D
5 C **6** C **7** B **8** A

2 **1** communication **2** anxiety
3 anger **4** irritation
5 ability **6** alertness
7 self-awareness **8** confidence
9 weight **10** subtlety/subtleties

3 **1** weakness **2** variety
3 credibility **4** certainty/certainties
5 persistence **6** complication
7 complaint **8** hunger

Vocabulary, page 116

A Word grid: Education

1 primary **2** resit
3 open **4** fail
5 education **6** subjects
7 state **8** Oxford
9 revise **10** professor

B Phrasal verbs with *turn*

1 down   2 up   3 into
4 on   5 out   6 off

C Expressions with *turn*

1 c   2 e   3 a   4 b
5 h   6 g   7 d   8 f

D Compound adjectives

1 *a British-trained doctor*
2 a Spanish-made car
3 a Russian-speaking guide
4 a London-based company
5 a French-owned supermarket chain
6 a ten-day cruise
7 a 29-year-old woman
8 a 650-page book
9 a four-hour film
10 a three-day conference

Language focus, page 117

Expressing purpose

1 1 c   2 e   3 a   4 f   5 h
    6 i   7 b   8 g   9 d

2

2 so that she wouldn't/so as not to/in order not to
   speak any Spanish.
3 in case it was cold there.
4 in case she didn't understand any English.
5 in order to see/so as to see/so that she could see
   the rest of the country.
6 so that she could read/in order to/so as to (be
   able to) read about the different places before
   visiting them.
7 so that her parents wouldn't worry about her. (in
   case her parents were worried about her.)
8 so that she doesn't/won't forget/in order not to
   forget/so as not to forget everything she learnt.
9 in case she decides to go back to Ireland next
   year.

Use of English, page 118

Transformations: Grammar revision

A Units 1–5

1 get used to living
2 feel like going
3 time the film starts
4 sing as well as he
5 such good English (that)
6 'd/had better not tell
7 don't/do not let us wear

B Units 6–9

1 not old enough to
2 had the house painted
3 it was raining heavily
4 to watch rather than play
5 first time I've/I have seen
6 aren't/are not likely to get
7 might have seen

C Units 10–15

1 he was being followed by
2 is said to be
3 had not broken down
4 if/whether he had been behaving
5 offered to carry his mother's
6 didn't/did not succeed in completing
7 I had not spent
8 so as not to/so that he wouldn't/would not

Open cloze

1 is   2 Each/Every   3 their
4 where   5 order   6 have
7 so   8 would   9 a/one
10 If   11 this   12 to

Word formation

1 inaccessible   2 written   3 suspicious
4 researchers   5 imprisoned   6 political
7 disappearance   8 fewer   9 unlikely
10 knowledge